Generative AI Art

A Beginner's Guide to 10x Your Output with Killer Text Prompts

Book 1 in the AI Text Prompt Engineering Series

Oliver Theobald

First Edition

Copyright © 2022 by Oliver Theobald

ISBN:

The contents of this book were last updated March 2024.

All rights reserved. No part of this publication may be reproduced, distributed, or transmitted in any form or by any means, including photocopying, recording, or other electronic or mechanical methods, without the prior written permission of the publisher, except in the case of brief quotations embodied in critical reviews and certain other non-commercial uses permitted by copyright law.

For inquiries, please contact the author at oliver.theobald@scatterplotpress.com

Please note that a video version of this book is available as a free mini-course at https://skl.sh/3u5Zd4X (limited to the first 1,000 readers).

TABLE OF CONTENTS

INTRODUCTION 5
A GENTLE INTRODUCTION TO AI 8
THE ART OF THE PROMPT 15
AI ART SOFTWARE 24
CRAIYON DEMONSTRATION 37
MIDJOURNEY DEMONSTRATION 41
AI-GENERATED PROMPTS 51
IMAGE PROMPTS & MASKING 57
FRAMING & LIGHTING 68
PARAMETERS 79
CONSISTENCY 86
REMIXING POPULAR STYLES OF ART 96
USEFUL TEXT PROMPTS 104
IMAGE RIGHTS 106
ETHICS, PRIVACY & ORIGINALITY 110
CONCLUSION 114
RECOMMENDED RESOURCES 116

INTRODUCTION

Within a matter of years, AI is set to radically transform the creative space. From creative writing to generative art, 3D rendering, video, speech, and music, we are set to witness advancements that will totally change the way we design and generate digital content.

The outputs that we can achieve from AI prompt-based software are already impressive and their outputs are only going to improve over time—just think in months, not years. In the creative writing and generative art fields, there are already dozens of credible companies offering advanced software tools that can generate magazine-worthy illustrations or consecutive paragraphs in virtually any genre of novel. Technology observers like Martin Shkreli and Kevin Rose have little doubt that we'll see a New York Times seller written by an AI within the next ten years. In the case of generative AI art, the results are mind-blowing and there's already debate over whether AI-generated art should be outright banned from art competitions.

As with previous trends, the surge in news and social media coverage is expected to bring fresh investment and talent into the field. The industry is poised to become the next frontier for engineering talent, presenting an exciting opportunity for people passionate about technological innovation. Whether it's developing software that enables users to unleash their creative potential or utilizing deep learning algorithms to detect AI-generated digital artwork, opportunities in the world of creative AI are available and abundant.

By leveraging the power of AI, software companies can also unlock unprecedented efficiency upgrades to existing software, while simultaneously revolutionizing the end-user experience, which is an important trend itself. Future versions of Photoshop or Microsoft Office will reduce the dependence on manual actions like click-and-drag and shift towards utilizing AI-powered text and voice prompts to guide the user's actions with accurate precision. Rather than hovering and pointing over the shoulder of an in-house designer, users will be able to highlight an area and change it by communicating directly with the software—all with no wait time. Users will dictate or type in the changes they want, and the AI will make it happen, instantly.

We are starting to see glimpses of this transition taking place with online graphic design tools such as Figma and Canva introducing new text-to-image apps on their platforms and Adobe adding generative AI technology to their existing software suite.

For other established players, these new developments will come as a wrecking ball through the creative industry as AI shoulders the low end of the market before working its way up the value chain. Diversified and dynamic gig-based marketplaces like Fiverr and Upwork have more room to maneuver but generic stock photography sites like Shutterstock face the threat of becoming entirely irrelevant in the face of AI-driven innovation.

Though AI-generated art holds a promising future, achieving widespread adoption will be a gradual process. The primary hurdle lies in its acceptance and adoption by companies and government organizations, and overcoming risks and ethical concerns, which are explored in Chapter 15. While many people have experimented with AI optimization for their profile pictures and shared their creations on social media, few are using AI as part of their professional workflow. Even fewer are actively exploring different platforms, learning about the unique strengths and limitations of each software option, and taking steps to enhance their skills in this emerging field of content creation.

For those early to the trend and curious to learn more about AI art, the following chapters will serve as your guide. With this book, you will gain a solid understanding of generative AI art as well as common techniques you can start implementing today.

Generative AI Art for Beginners covers all the basics of AI art, from its technological underpinnings to the practical possibilities of new software applications. It explains what text prompts are, how they work, and why they matter. This book also provides an overview of key topics such as framing, lighting, and image parameters, as well as the limits of AI art creation. Additionally, the book provides guidance on choosing and using AI art software and other resources, as well as ethical considerations when working with technology in this field. By the end of this reading, you will have a comprehensive understanding of how to effectively incorporate AI software into your creative content stack and gain insight into the future direction of this rapidly evolving industry.

Given that software development is moving so quickly, the chapters in this book will focus on the key concepts and theoretical considerations behind creating AI art, such as text prompt construction, framing, consistency, and image masking, rather than in-depth instructions on how to use and navigate the user interface (UI) for each software service.

Lastly, it's important to understand that creating AI art doesn't require any specialized programming knowledge or even much talent for design. With the right software and guidance, anyone can quickly become a master at creating AI-generated artwork. That said, constructing a good prompt requires practical experience, including knowledge of special techniques, and some domain expertise in your subject matter to match your artistic vision. This is a skill that can be honed, leading to a deepened understanding of art and design along the way.

That said, let's get started with generative AI art!

A GENTLE INTRODUCTION TO AI

An art revolution of transformative proportions is underway. AI-powered tools like DALL-E, Midjourney, Stable Diffusion, Craiyon, and a slew of other new software names are empowering individuals to effortlessly produce top-tier art and visuals in a matter of seconds. Even more impressive is the fact that these tools can be operated using simple text descriptions, without the need for coding expertise or prior artistic experience. Yet, to understand and maximize the utility of these software offerings, a foundational comprehension of AI is important, especially in understanding the potential limits and drawbacks of AI-generated content.

Artificial intelligence, commonly abbreviated as "AI", has gained significant traction in recent years. At its core, AI facilitates the creation of machines that can learn, problem-solve, and provide appropriate responses, including the ability to interact with humans and act independently. This is achieved by first teaching the computer how to recognize patterns in pre-existing data and then training it to make independent decisions based on new input data. This transformational technology has revolutionized problem-solving, making it possible to address challenges that were previously insurmountable, time-consuming, or beyond human capacity.

As new algorithms continue to be developed and techniques are refined, AI technology holds the potential to shape the future in numerous ways and revolutionize many aspects of our lives, spanning healthcare, transportation, content creation, music, and software. With boundless opportunities and possibilities, AI is an exciting and rapidly evolving field, with many more exciting advancements on the horizon that are set to transform our personal and professional lives. Examples include searching for songs using text descriptions (i.e. "early 2000s pop with a brash and uplifting chorus") and hiring an AI narrator trained to speak in your own voice. For a glimpse of the future, check out theresanaiforthat.com, which lists newly released AI-powered software offerings.

Lastly, it's important to remember that AI is not one single technique, but, rather, a broad umbrella that spans a collection of techniques. This includes natural language processing (NLP) which makes it possible to understand human language, image recognition to identify objects in an image or video, as well as robotics, computer vision, and machine learning. The techniques used for generative AI art are based on a combination of natural language processing, image recognition, and machine learning.

Machine learning

As the backbone of AI, machine learning gives computers the ability to learn without being explicitly programmed. To be specific, decisions are generated by deciphering relationships and patterns from data using probabilistic reasoning, trial and error, and other computationally-intensive techniques. This means that the output of the decision model is determined by the contents of the input data rather than any pre-set rules defined by a human programmer. The human programmer is still responsible for piping data into the model, selecting an appropriate algorithm, and tweaking its learning parameters, but ultimately the machine and developer operate a layer apart in contrast to traditional programming.

There are several categories of machine learning techniques, including unsupervised learning and reinforcement learning, but let's focus on supervised learning, which is the most relevant to generative AI.

Supervised Learning

Supervised learning involves extracting patterns from known examples and using that extracted insight to engineer a repeatable outcome. Well before the advent of machine learning, humans employed this technique to deconstruct and reverse-engineer everything from automobiles to gunpowder weapons. The Japanese car manufacturer Toyota used this approach to design its first car prototype. Rather than design a unique process from scratch, Toyota created its first vehicle prototype after dissembling a Chevrolet car in the corner of their family-run loom business. By observing the finished car (output) and then pulling apart its individual components (input), Toyota's engineers deconstructed the design process kept secret by Chevrolet in America.

Figure 1: A representation of how Toyota built its first car model, Toyota Commemorative Museum of Industry and Technology

This technique of studying a known combination of inputs to create a known output is replicated in supervised learning. The machine learning model analyzes and deciphers the relationship between input and output data to learn the underlying patterns. In the case of AI art, the algorithm looks at images that are labeled with text descriptions such as "car", "Toyota", "building a car", "wooden car frame", "front of car", etc, and with more data and more experience, it begins to learn what a constitutes a car and other objects based on millions of training examples. This is what is meant by giving the computer the ability to learn without being explicitly programmed.

By decoding complex patterns from the labeled data, the model finds connections without human help, and in the case of AI art, it is using NLP to understand the relationship between text (input) and images (output). After analyzing enough examples, a trained model is formed based on an algorithmic equation. Using the patterns learned from the training data, the model can take a new input in the form of text and generate an output in the form of an image.

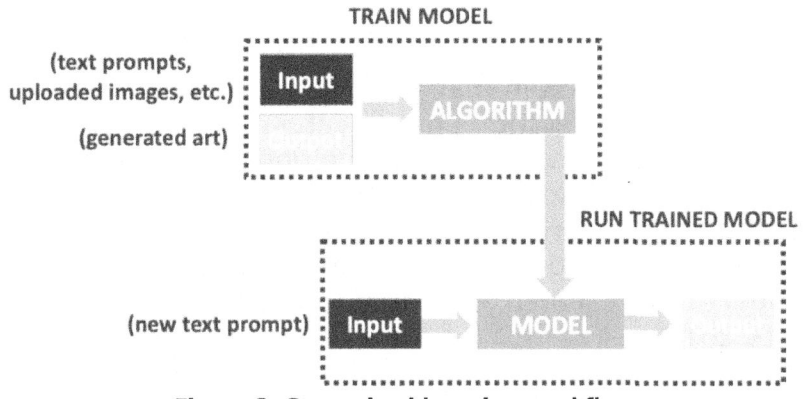

Figure 2: Supervised learning workflow

Natural Language Processing

While AI has clearly made a significant impression on individuals and investors, it is natural language processing that is enabling many of the ground-breaking possibilities within the creative space. NLP shares some similarities with machine learning, particularly supervised learning in the analysis of established patterns, but it represents a distinctive subfield of AI that combines elements of machine learning with the study of human language and semantics.

Inspired by linguistics, NLP was originally designed for parsing text in databases via coding rules systems, but over time, it merged with common algorithms from machine learning to evolve into a novel and specialized field of computational linguistics. NLP revolves around analyzing human language, placing less emphasis on numerical values or quantitative problem-solving, which are typically the focus of other subfields related to artificial intelligence. This is accomplished by creating models that scrutinize text and speech to determine their meaning. For instance, if you ask an NLP model a question like, "**What's the weather like tomorrow?**", it can assist in interpreting the query and delivering an appropriate response. This breakthrough has proven to be a significant achievement, enabling users to rapidly obtain information or generate a desired image using just a few carefully-selected words.

NLP, though, is not a new discovery. It has been around for decades and is used in many familiar applications including Siri, Google Assistant, and Facebook, which use NLP techniques including voice recognition (using speech-to-text conversion) and retrieving text information to fulfill users' search queries. What sets this era apart is the emergence of a large language model called GPT developed by OpenAI, a research institution founded by Sam Altman in late 2015.

GPT

Most of the recent breakthroughs in generative AI have been enabled by an advanced machine learning model for studying language and generating text called GPT-3. GPT stands for Generative Pre-trained Transformer, and because it's the third version of this model, it's called GPT-3. (Note that this model has since been succeeded by GPT-4.)

After training on 570 gigabytes of text information (gathered and crawled from the Internet, along with selected texts such as articles from Wikipedia), GPT-3 has been developed to generate art, music, poetry, and prose using text-based prompts.

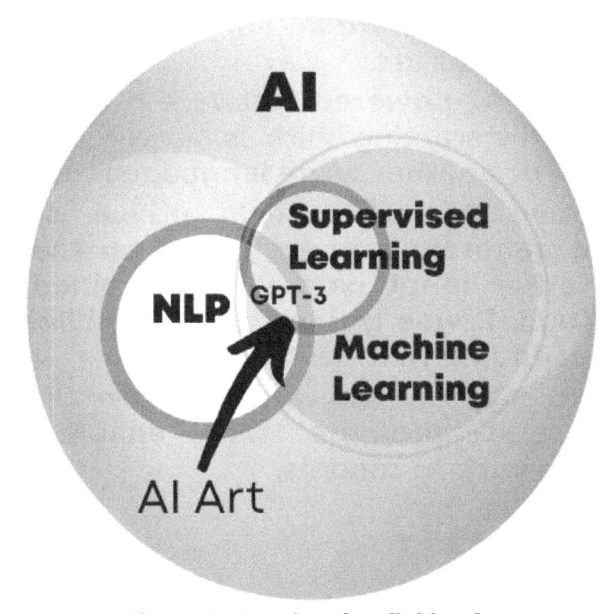

Figure 3: Overlapping fields of AI

From abstract painting to multiple-exposure photography, large language models like GPT have revolutionized the way we think about content and creative experimentation. By combining the creativity of humans with the power of machines, generative AI art provides a space for individuals to unleash their imagination and experiment with artistic concepts that previously required creative talent and technical training to achieve. This technology also enables creators to explore new creative possibilities and create high-quality visualizations, text, and animations that would be time-consuming and expensive to produce using traditional methods.

This chapter has briefly introduced a number of advanced technical concepts and while it's not essential to have prior knowledge to start creating AI

art, having a basic understanding will help you recognize the limitations and inclinations of large language models. If you are interested in delving deeper, I have additional books available that cover machine learning in more detail, but for now, the key points to remember are:

1) Most of the AI-powered software that you will be working and interacting with is powered under the hood by GPT or another large language model.

2) Generative AI art models utilize supervised learning to generate outputs based on the images, text, and other input data it was trained on. For instance, DALL-E was trained on 650 million images with corresponding text descriptions.

In the next chapter, we will dive into the various forms of text prompts that enable you to communicate with AI models.

3

THE ART OF THE PROMPT

To produce generative AI art, you will first need to write what's called a **text prompt**, which serves as an instruction to the AI model, outlining what it is you want to create. A prompt can be as simple as **a person sitting at a café** or even a single word like **café.** The AI model will then do its best to generate an image based on the text prompt provided.

Figure 4: A person sitting at a café (Midjourney)

Similar to how individuals have their own unique approach of using keywords and phrases to search on Google or other search engines, there is no set methodology or code for writing text prompts. This means a prompt can be anything from a list of words separated by commas (i.e. **bear, tree**), a fragment of a sentence (i.e. **bear under a tree**), an imperative (i.e. **sketch a bear next to a tree**), or a full sentence (i.e. **A sketch of a bear sitting under a tree.**). Correct grammar isn't necessary as long as the instructions can be clearly understood, and in most cases, the easier your prompt is to understand, the better.

It's essential to use natural language as that's the language the AI is trained on. Natural language refers to human languages, such as everyday conversation or what you use to write a text message, as opposed to an artificial language such as a programming language. This means you should communicate to the AI program like it's a human and avoid using artificial languages like CSS and Python to write your text prompts. However, keep in mind that there are some exceptions, including the specialized syntax that comes with the AI software program, such as **/imagine** in the case of Midjourney (the first word of your text prompt) and other special commands for dictating the weighting, size, and structural aspects of the image. We will discuss and explore these special commands in later chapters.

How to Create an Effective Prompt

Most AI software programs come equipped with a built-in feature that enables users to apply variations, allowing them to modify or riff on what the model has already generated. Often, it can take numerous variations before achieving the desired look and feel for the target image or artwork. However, the more specific the original text prompt is, the more specific the outcome will be, and the fewer iterations needed to achieve the desired result.

At the start of this chapter, we looked at the simple text prompt in the form of **a person sitting at a café**. Although this prompt contains enough information for the

AI to generate a relevant image, there is room to refine this prompt and generate a more precise output.

This is where *modifiers* come in. While your base prompt will typically describe one or more objects and their relationship within that scene, a modifier adds additional instructions regarding the stylistic design you want the AI model to take, helping to generate a more precise and nuanced output.

A person sitting at a café in the style of an 1920's art deco poster

⬆   ⬆

Base prompt   **Modifier**

If we take the original base prompt of **a person sitting at a café**, we can add a modifier in the form of **a person sitting at a café <u>in the style of a 1920's art deco poster</u>**. This will produce a more nuanced result when compared to the original output that used a more simple and generic version of the prompt.

Figure 5: A person sitting at a café in the style of a 1920's art deco poster (Midjourney)

We can also go back and edit the original prompt to add more details. Let's update it to the following: **a distinguished middle-aged man** sitting at a **Viennese coffee house** in the style of an art deco poster **from the 1920s**.

Figure 6: A distinguished middle-aged man sitting at a Viennese coffee house in the style of an art deco poster from the 1920s (Midjourney)

Keep in mind that most software programs come with a character limit. For DALL-E, the prompt cannot be more than 400 characters, which is more than enough for just about anything you would need to create. However, if you are precise with your prompt and you curate the right words, then sometimes, less is more. In fact, you can generate decent results using just emojis—depending on which AI software program you are using. Additionally, a simple description such as **art deco poster** contains a number of pre-defined characteristics (i.e. rich colors, lavish ornamentation, geometric shapes, and the actual material/medium of the art in the form of paper and rectangle in shape) that you would otherwise need to list and define separately.

Additionally, artistic movements such as art deco or a decade like the 1990s will not only impact the style of the illustration but also the fashion, architecture, and other materials depicted in the illustration (unless otherwise defined). Conversely, if you encounter problems recreating a specific style using broad terms such as **art deco** or **grunge**, you can incorporate additional details such as the location (i.e. Wall Street, New York), weather conditions, time of day, and historical, political, economic, or social context (i.e. Occupy Wall Street, September 11, the Global Financial Crisis, COVID-19 pandemic, etc.) to achieve the desired effect.

For AI-generated photography, you can borrow domain-specific terminology to define everything from shutter speed to lens choice, lighting, and framing, or bundle these attributes into a known style of photography such as action shot, National Geographic cover, Japanese photobooth (purikura), selfie, or Vogue photo shoot. Likewise, if you want to create a specific visual style, then you should understand the framing (angle), lighting, and materials for replicating that given style of photography.

As you refine your ability to articulate visual art through language, you'll cultivate a skill that unveils new insights into specialized terminology and subject areas, resulting in fun discoveries as you explore different rabbit holes. With experience, you may even catch yourself narrating scenes in your head as you watch a movie before testing those descriptions as text prompts using Midjourney or DALL-E. With practice, this skill can become second nature, allowing you to generate increasingly refined prompts and expanding your awareness of artistic techniques in everyday life.

In addition to becoming more articulate with your text prompts, you also want to confirm details and the accuracy of your art. This requires having a strong understanding of the subject matter and ensuring that the details in your art are as precise and representative as possible.

To generate an image of a medieval knight, it helps to have an understanding of the fashion, social class system, and weapons used during that period, for example. This includes knowledge of famous medieval knights and their attire in order to create a more precise text prompt. For example, a Templar knight dressed in white with a red cross on his uniform would look vastly different from an

English knight from an earlier period, who donned their own unique crest and fashion. Similarly, if you are producing a backstreet scene in Osaka for a Japanese-speaking audience, then you may want to confirm that the Japanese characters used in the backdrop are accurate (which in almost all cases they are not!).

Figure 7: The characters (kanji) in this image are unidentifiable (Midjourney)

It's important to keep in mind that AI models will make mistakes, including simple tasks such as generating eligible text and more complex tasks such as creating realistic photos and depicting human faces. In addition, it's important to keep in mind that the AI model is not omniscient like a genie or a god-like figure, its knowledge is solely derived from the data it was trained on. DALL-E, for example, was initially trained on 650 million images but it's not equipped to identify an exhaustive array of subjects. Thus, expecting the AI model to accurately reveal the exact face of Satoshi Nakamoto (founder of Bitcoin) or Banksy (anonymous artist) is impossible unless there are existing visual references in the model's training data.

To obtain new knowledge, the model has to be retrained. As a result, it may take time for the AI model to catch up with recent events and it may not be reliable at creating art related to new trends, subjects, or words.

Next, your prompts need to be context-specific and well-defined. Using vague or ambiguous terms can lead to unintended or incomplete results. For instance, using the word **me** in your text prompt won't give the AI any information about your physical appearance. Even if you are famous and your portraits and images are freely accessible in the public domain, you will still need to state the precise name of the individual (which in this case is your own name). You may also need to provide additional context to avoid confusion and prevent any mix-up with others who bear the same name, i.e. Michael Jordan the actor and Michael Jordan the basketball player. Having emphasized the importance of specific and precise text prompt engineering, sometimes it's valuable to allow the AI model to assume a more creative role. By using a more open-ended or less constrained prompt, you will empower the AI to explore the potential interpretations of your description. This technique is useful when there are few references in the real world or when you're unsure of what something should look like, such as a virtual football stadium built in the metaverse.

Finally, due to randomness built into the AI model, using the same text prompt twice will usually produce different results, so you may want to test the same text prompt multiple times and explore the full array of potential options.

Figure 8: Virtual football stadium built in the metaverse (Midjourney)

AI ART SOFTWARE

As the field continues to evolve at a rapid pace, more and more software programs are emerging, each with its own unique set of features, styles, and capabilities. This means that each AI software will produce drastically different results using the exact same text prompt. Midjourney, for instance, leans towards a more artistic style, while DALL-E tends to be more conservative and literal. If you are seeking to achieve a specific style or outcome, you may need to switch to a different software solution or provide more detailed instructions in your text prompt in order to override the natural style or bias of that particular software.

Overall, by understanding the default style and the different capabilities between popular software options, you can choose the best one to meet your needs and achieve your creative vision based on the task at hand.

Let's now take a closer look at some of the leading software options available for producing generative AI art. In this chapter, we will examine a variety of different options, including both paid and free, and explore the various pros and cons of each option.

DALL-E | openai.com/dall-e-3

DALL-E, or DALL-E 3 (its latest version), has taken the world by storm since its release in 2022. Developed by OpenAI and powered by the GPT large language model, DALL-E was the first software program to reveal the possibilities of text-to-image technology.

Named after surrealist artist Salvador Dalí and Pixar's WALL-E, DALL-E is capable of understanding complex sentences, involving multiple objects and their attributes, including color, shape, size, style, lighting, and location. Using text prompts, you can quickly generate an image of a red rectangle next to a blue triangle or generate more abstract, fantastical images, such as a pink cloud with two eyes and a mouth.

Figure 9: Pink cloud with two eyes and a mouth (DALL-E)

After signing up for a new account with OpenAI, you can type in your text prompt or upload an image to edit directly or generate variations. Images that you generate using DALL-E are then saved to your account for convenient access later.

Figure 10: DALL-E's clean user interface and image generator tool

One of DALL-E's best features is the image uploader tool, which is useful for manipulating existing art and design elements to create novel combinations. As an example, you can take an existing photograph and add a unique element, such as a flying pig or a robot arm.

After an initial invite-only beta release, DALL-E is now available for users in most (but not all) countries. After signing up, you will have free access to DALL-E 2. To use the latest version, DALL-E 3, you will need to subscribe to one of their current pricing plans. Note that pricing plans and their benefits are subject to change over time.

While the landscape is changing rapidly, DALL-E is very simple to use and offers more features than most other AI software on the market. While the artistic capabilities are not as impressive as newer software competitors, it is definitely worth testing and comparing with other popular options such as Midjourney.

Midjourney | www.midjourney.com

Midjourney stands out among the first generation of AI software, partly for the fact that it's built on top of Discord. Unlike most generative AI art software such as DALL-E, Midjourney was not released as a standalone web application with instant access. Instead, it is available as a bot that can be accessed through the popular chat app

Discord (available as a desktop or mobile app), which is prominent in the gaming and crypto space. This makes the user experience of Midjourney unique and more complex compared to other software options.

On top of this, there are thousands of other Midjourney users creating and modifying their AI art on the Midjourney Discord channel at any given time. Although the constant flood of text prompts inside the chat rooms can be distracting, the shared work environment does offer an opportunity to gain inspiration and observe the workflow and art of other users.

After joining the Midjourney channel on Discord, you will be able to start creating images using the **/imagine** command followed by your text prompt. Note that you will also need to purchase one of multiple paid subscription plans for Midjourney based on your needs.

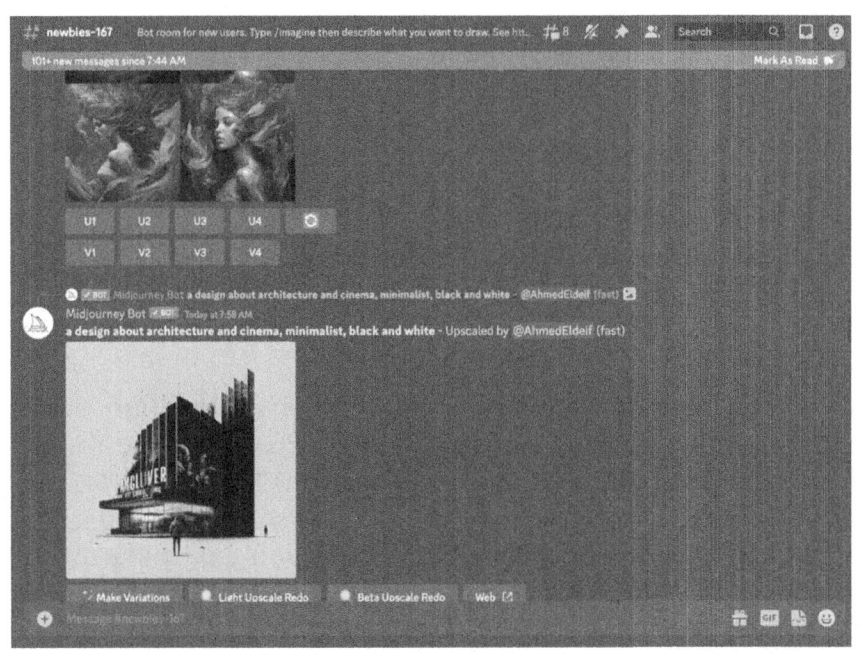

Figure 11: Midjourney's Discord channel which doubles as its image generation platform

In terms of its artistic output, Midjourney leans towards more abstract and surrealist designs and is particularly good at outputting futuristic or cyberpunk-style art. However, recent upgrades to Midjourney have drastically improved its ability to produce realistic photography and human subjects. Overall, the precision and image quality of Midjourney since its fourth and fifth version updates, taking place in 2023, make it hard to compete with. If you still experience a bias towards abstract or unrealistic designs, then you may need to add the terms **realistic**, **photo-realistic**, and **realism** to your text prompts.

Midjourney's other advantage is that it offers an advanced range of parameters to customize your generated artwork, including aspect ratio, resolution, image quality, and complexity, which are covered in Chapter 10. It also provides tools for integrating animation and motion into your visuals to help them stand out even more.

While it has a steeper learning curve than its website-based peers, Midjourney is well worth the time investment for users willing to learn and experiment. Personally, Midjourney is one of three software solutions I use on a regular basis and one of two platforms where I have a paid subscription account (the other being DALL-E).

Craiyon | www.craiyon.com

Formally known as DALL-E mini, Craiyon was created by team members involved with DALL-E, meaning there is some cross-over in terms of product development and history between the two products.

The user interface for Craiyon is delivered through a web browser that you can access on your PC or mobile device. There is also a mobile app available for Android users.

The key advantage of Craiyon is that it's simple to use and offers unlimited usage. Using Craiyon, you can generate art in minutes and download those images for free. You can create as much art as you want, and, in fact, you don't even have to sign up for an account. Craiyon now also offers a useful background remover tool.

The downside is that the results are slow to generate (up to two minutes) and low in resolution. Also, as the images you create using this software are for non-commercial use only,

Craiyon is not intended for commercial design scenarios. Instead, Craiyon is more suitable for creating fun images to share with friends and family or for general experimentation.

Note that Craiyon also asks users to "Please credit craiyon.com for the images" that are used publicly.

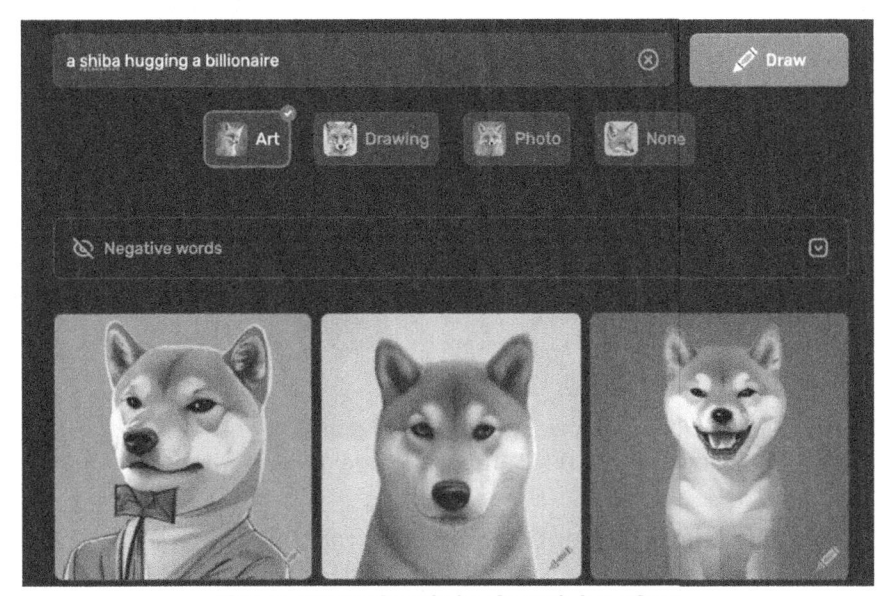

Figure 12: Craiyon's basic web interface

Stable Diffusion | www.stablediffusionweb.com

Stable Diffusion is another powerful tool for artists and designers. Unlike DALL-E and Midjourney, Stable Diffusion has an open-source policy that lets you bypass blocked content restrictions that you might encounter using other AI software.

With no account signup required and fast image processing (approximately 10 seconds), you can start generating images immediately. The downside of its simple user interface and the lack of sign-in options is that you can't easily view images that you previously generated. Instead, you will need to regularly save the image results to your computer.

Stable Diffusion Playground

Just enter your prompt and click the generate button.
No code required to generate your image!

Due to the large number of users, the server may experience problems. If you encounter an error, please try again.

a shiba hugging a billionaire   Generate image

Figure 13: Stable Diffusion image generator tool

Stable Diffusion currently lacks the features of its software rivals, such as image uploading and aspect ratio controls. However, the developers recently added a negative prompt box and new features will continue to be added.

On the plus side, Stable Diffusion is fast, free to use, and the results are far superior to Craiyon and other free AI art software.

In terms of its artistic style, Stable Diffusion is similar to Midjourney and favors a more abstract and surrealist style of artistic expression. As with many other software programs, it does tend to struggle with capturing symmetry in human faces.

StarryAI | www.starryai.com

StarryAI is an AI art generator app and web application that lets you generate NFTs (non-fungible tokens) using text prompts to transform your words into works of art

30

recorded on the blockchain. The platform allows users to publish NFTs on different blockchains including Ethereum and the Binance Smart Chain, enabling NFTs to be easily distributed and traded on various blockchain networks.

The StarryAI design studio lets you choose between their Argo (standard) and Altair (more dream-like and abstract) AI models and comes with a good number of features including image uploader (for prompt inspiration), canvas size, the design choice between realistic or artistic, and runtime (a trade-off between using more credits and achieving better results).

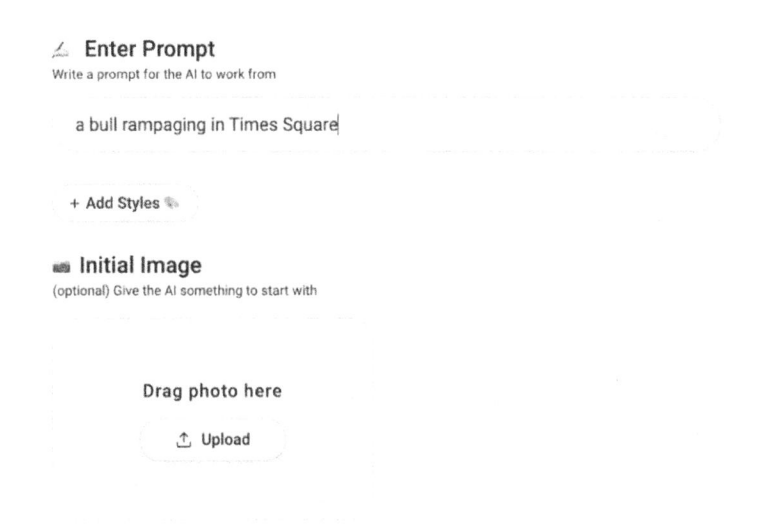

✎ **Enter Prompt**
Write a prompt for the AI to work from

a bull rampaging in Times Square

+ Add Styles

Initial Image
(optional) Give the AI something to start with

Drag photo here

↑ Upload

Figure 14: StarryAI image generator tool

Importantly, StarryAI gives you full ownership of your creations, which you can use for your next creative project, print, share on social media, or sell as an NFT, giving artists an extra avenue to monetize their creativity. Note that while your art creations belong to you and you can do whatever you like with them, you are still subject to copyright laws in your jurisdiction and you may need special permission from the copyright owner for the use of any input image(s).

Using StarryAI, you can generate up to five artworks for free daily, without watermarks. However, you will need to buy credits to enjoy full usage. StarryAI is also available as an app on iOS and Android.

Nightcafe | creator.nightcafe.studios

Nightcafe offers a similar design suite and pricing system (pay-per-credit) as StarryAI, allowing you to generate up to five artworks for free daily.

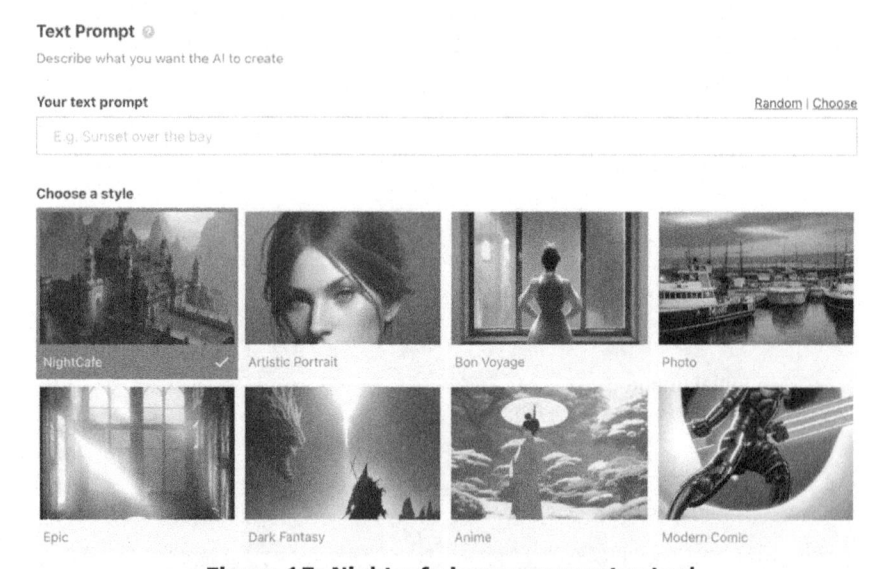

Figure 15: Nightcafe image generator tool

Whereas StarryAI focuses on NFT creation, Nightcafe lets you print your creations on thick and durable matte paper as a poster and have them mailed to your house.

Similar to StarryAI, Nightcafe provides extra settings including artistic style, aspect ratio, prompt weight, and image resolution.

Synthesys X | synthesys.io

As a browser extension for Google Chrome, Synthesys X gives users the ability to quickly generate variations of existing images without the need for text prompts or special inputs. By right-clicking on any image you find online and selecting **"Replicate the image"**, you can generate royalty-free images that are relevant and similar to the original image.

According to the startup's co-founder, Oliver Goodwin, the mechanics of the image generation work by analyzing the original image, translating it into a text description, and then creating variations based on that text input (similar to other AI art software).[1] This allows the Synthesys X Chrome extension to create unique images without reproducing or manipulating the original image.

This approach is useful for creating small variations or tweaks to existing designs, rather than generating entirely new images from scratch. One drawback of Synthesys X is that it doesn't offer the same level of creative control as other AI art software, since the user is limited to modifying existing images rather than generating new ones based on text prompts. However, it can be a useful tool for quickly iterating on ideas or exploring different variations of an existing design.

While it's still early to give a verdict on the legality or the ethical grounds of this new plug-in, it's easy to use and offers something different from other software currently available.

Figure 16: Using Synthesys X to generate a hamburger using stock photography as a prompt

---

[1] Synthesys X, Product Hunt, www.producthunt.com/posts/synthesys-x, accessed January 12, 2023.

Art Examples

Text prompt: cute boy wearing glasses, curly hair, pixar style, 4k

Craiyon

DALL-E

Stable Diffusion

StarryAI

Nightcafe

Midjourney

CRAIYON DEMONSTRATION

To create our first AI-generated design, let's explore Craiyon.com, which is one of the quickest and easiest options to start your journey with generative AI art.

In terms of getting started, there are far fewer steps to creating your first art piece than Midjourney and DALL-E. There is no sign-up, no verification, and nothing to download. In fact, all you need to do is go to craiyon.com, enter your text prompt in the search bar and click the orange "**Draw**" button.

You will need to wait 1-2 minutes for the model to generate your request. Once it's done, Craiyon will display nine options in a three-by-three grid for you to choose from.

Figure 17: Chewbacca style puppy created on Craiyon.com

Next, we can test some of Craiyon's basic features, including negative prompting and style design. For example, we can dictate elements we don't want to include in the image using negative prompting, such as **mouth open**. In terms of style design, we can select from Art, Drawing, Photo, and None.

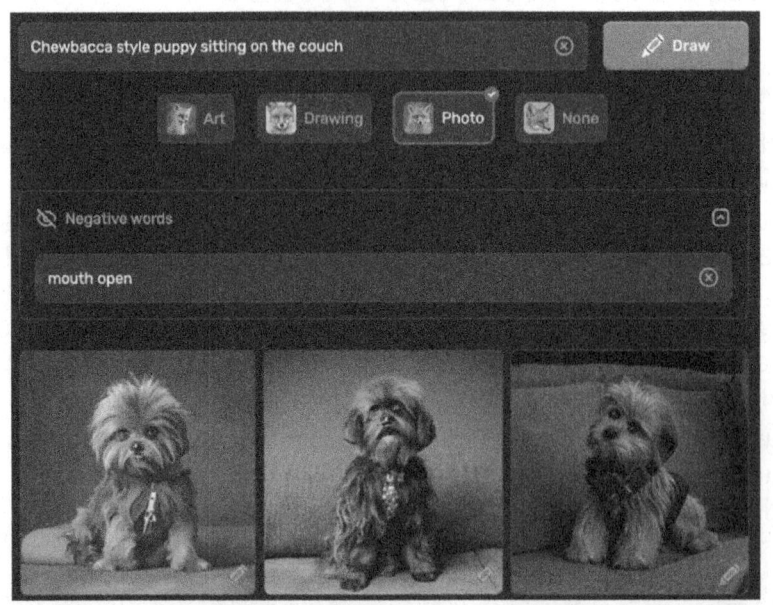

Figure 18: Using negative prompting and the Photo style option on Craiyon.com

By switching the art style to "Photo" and using negative prompting, we get the results shown in Figure 18.

In general, the quality of the results is not bad, as you can see in Figure 17 and 18. The image quality, meanwhile, is passable but not ideally optimized for production level—with the image resolution much lower than its competitors including Midjourney and Stable Diffusion.

In the past, the software also struggled with rendering human faces as you can see in Figure 19, but it is beginning to improve as we can see in Figure 20.

Figure 19: A photorealistic image of a TV anchor presenting the news (craiyon.com) generated in March 2023.

Figure 20: A photorealistic image of a TV anchor presenting the news (craiyon.com) generated in March 2024.

Regarding the other drawbacks of this free service, if we look at the tools and features, there are not as many options as Midjourney, DALL-E and other software for

39

remixing your art, uploading an image as input data, or controlling specific details about the art including aspect ratios. This makes Craiyon a fun tool to share with friends and for creating mocks-up, but not suitable for enterprise needs and commercial usage.

MIDJOURNEY DEMONSTRATION

In this chapter, we will explore Midjourney, which is one of the most popular software options for creating AI art.

In order to use Midjourney, you should be at least 13 years old and meet the minimum age of digital consent in your country. If you aren't old enough or you have younger family members who want to use Midjourney, a parent or guardian can agree to the terms on the user's behalf. Note that Midjourney takes an active stance in ensuring its platform maintains a PG-13 and family-friendly environment. This includes the following warning on their website: "Do not create images or use text prompts that are inherently disrespectful, aggressive, or otherwise abusive." They also state, "No adult content or gore… Please avoid making visually shocking or disturbing content. We will block some text inputs automatically."

In addition, you might encounter instances where specific words or phrases are restricted, preventing you from creating images by using them in your prompt. If you see the red cross emoji pop up next to your work, interpret this as a warning about your content's suitability. In other situations, your content may be deleted from view or just not produced at all. You can self-police your content by deleting it yourself using the red cross emoji reaction within Discord. This will delete the image from public view.

If you are producing adult, horror, or content not suitable for minors, you may want to look for other software solutions like Stable Diffusion, which is open-source and allows you to create whatever you want.

Getting Started

To get started, you first need to register a Discord account at discord.com. Discord is a popular instant messaging social platform and is free to join. After registering for a free account, you can choose to download Discord onto your personal computer as an app or open Discord directly from your web browser.

After you have completed setting up your Discord account, you can navigate to the midjourney.com website and click on the "**Join the Beta**" button displayed on the homepage. You will be automatically redirected to Discord, either within your web browser or directly to the desktop app (if already downloaded).

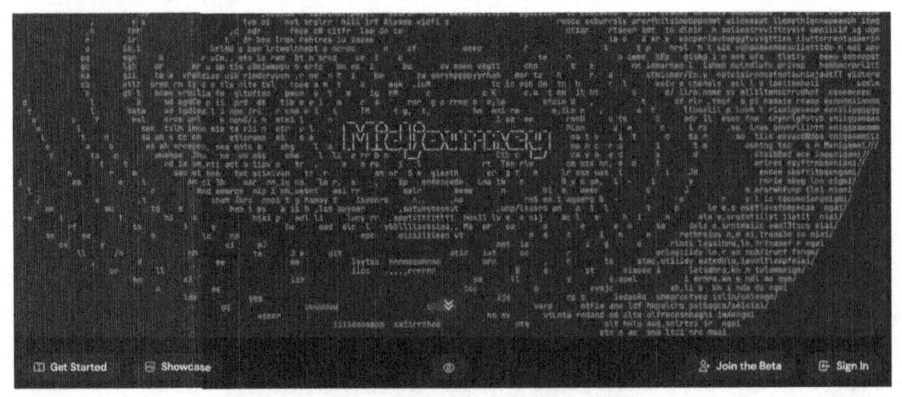

Figure 21: Midjourney homepage

Once you are inside Discord, you will need to confirm that you are inside the official Midjourney channel. This means you should see a green tick when you hover your mouse over the Midjourney icon. Once confirmed, you can check out the Midjourney welcome message, which includes key and up-to-date practical information about the service.

Figure 22: Make sure you see a green tick badge next to the name of the Midjourney channel

Step 1: Go to the Midjourney Discord channel

Navigate to one of the "**newbies**" channels within the Midjourney Discord server on the left-hand side, under "**NEWCOMER ROOMS**". Note that there are many newbies channels and you don't need to enter one specific channel. If forced to choose, simply look for a channel with as little activity as possible to reduce the level of background chaos.

If you don't see any newbies channels, confirm that you are on the official Midjourney server or try restarting the Discord app or webpage.

Figure 23: Selecting a newbie room on Discord to create your image

Step 2: Initiate image generation

Once you are inside a newbies channel, you can check out what other users are creating and take note of their text prompts and choice of keywords.

When you are ready to start creating, you can click on the chat box tab at the bottom of the chat feed and type in **/imagine**. As you start typing, you will see a tab pop up above the text, which you need to click on to confirm that you want to create a new image.

Figure 24: Initiating the /imagine command to create your first prompt

Step 3: Enter full text prompt

Enter the full text prompt you wish to use. For this demonstration, I will use **Barack Obama playing bass guitar** with no specific style defined.

(Please note that Midjourney asks you to respect their "Content and Moderation policy" by keeping content PG-13 and avoiding upsetting imagery.)

Figure 25: Creating a text prompt using Midjourney inside Discord

Once you are satisfied with your prompt, you can press "**Enter**" on your keyboard or click the send button (just like sending a message on a chat app). This action will send your request to the Midjourney Bot, which will start generating your image.

Based on the text prompt you entered, the Midjourney Bot will generate four options, which will take a minute or less to deliver. The results will start out looking fuzzy but will gradually become more refined as the progress indicator reaches full completion.

Step 4: Create a new variation

Once the progress indicator has reached 100%, you will see a two-by-2 grid of finished images and two rows of buttons below.

Figure 26: Midjourney image results

The top row of buttons is for upscaling your images. Upscaling an image means generating a larger pixel version of the selected image, approximately 1024x1024, which will make your images look crisper and automatically add additional details to give your image a polished finish. You should think of the initial two-by-two grid of images as mockups provided by the AI model, which is saving its resources for later iterations. The upscaled version can be thought of as the final version, which is ready for use and up to production level in terms of image quality.

Note that the numbered buttons **U1** (top-left), **U2** (top-right), **U3** (bottom-left), and **U4** (bottom-right) each correspond to an individual image, starting on the left and moving to the right. If you wish to upscale the first image, for example, then all you need to do is click on **U1**.

The next option is to create variations of your art using the second row of buttons. Creating variations will generate four new images that are different but still similar in overall style and composition to the image you selected from the four mockup options. Again, the **V1**, **V2**, **V3**, and **V4** buttons each correspond to an individual image from the two-by-two grid above.

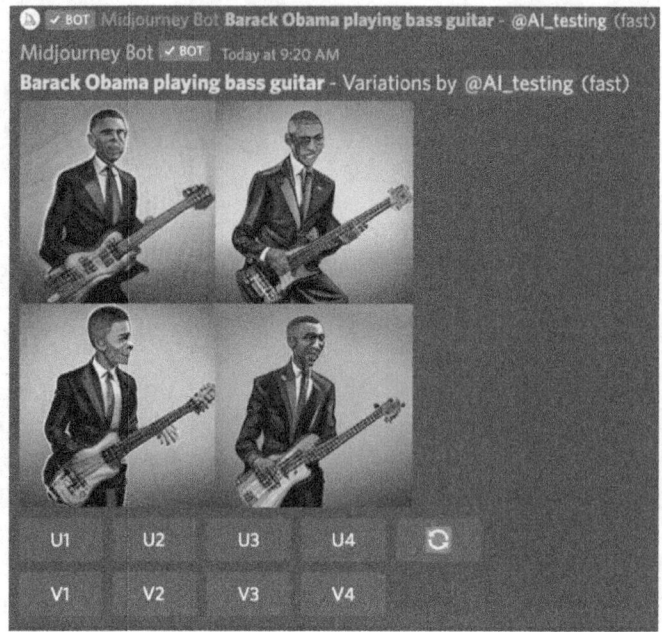

Figure 27: Midjourney image variation results for V1 (variation 1)

For this demonstration, let's go ahead and click on **VI** and see what the Midjourney Bot generates as a variation.

After clicking **V1**, the Midjourney Bot has come back with a two-by-two grid of variations based on the original image we selected.

Step 5: Upscale your image

46

Next, let's try an Upscale by clicking on **U4** which maps to the image in the bottom right position of the two-by-two grid.

At this point, you may need to scroll up to find your new output among the other images that are being generated every few seconds by other Midjourney users. This is one of the downsides of using Midjourney and Discord as it can be hard to find your own art sometimes!

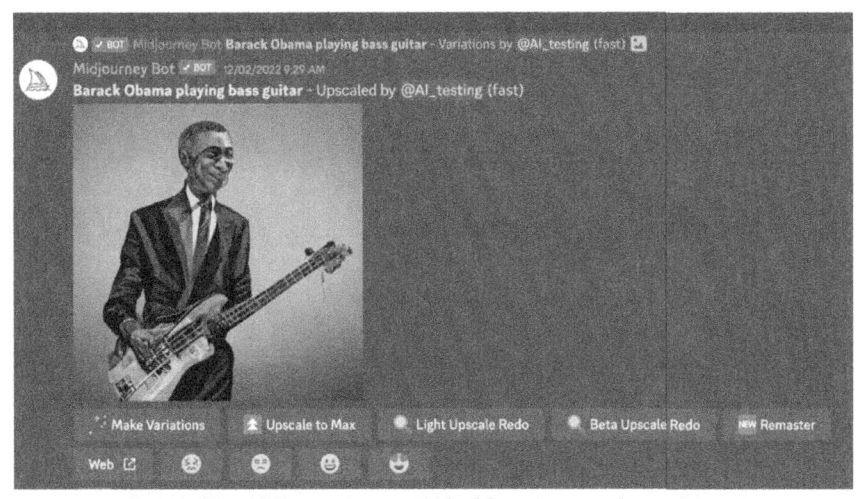

Figure 28: Midjourney upscaled image results using U4

Here we can see that the Midjourney Bot has generated an upscaled version of the original image. This new version contains more detail and depth compared to the mockup version we selected, and overall, looks a lot better!

After upscaling the image, there are a few more options displayed below. The first option (**Make Variations**) is to generate variations of the image results as we did before—think of this as telling the AI to riff or remix what's been created so far. The second option is **Upscale to Max**, which upscales the image to an even larger resolution of approximately 1664x1664. **Light Upscale Redo**, meanwhile, upscales the image again without adding as much detail.

Step 6: Save your image

In terms of saving the image for future use, there are a few options available. One option is to send the image to yourself by asking the Midjourney Bot to send you a direct message in Discord containing the final image. To do this, click on the add reaction icon in the top right (above the image) and search for the envelope emoji by typing in "envelope". After clicking on the envelope emoji (✉), Midjourney will automatically send the image to you in a separate message window, which you can find at the top of the left-hand sidebar containing all your direct messages.

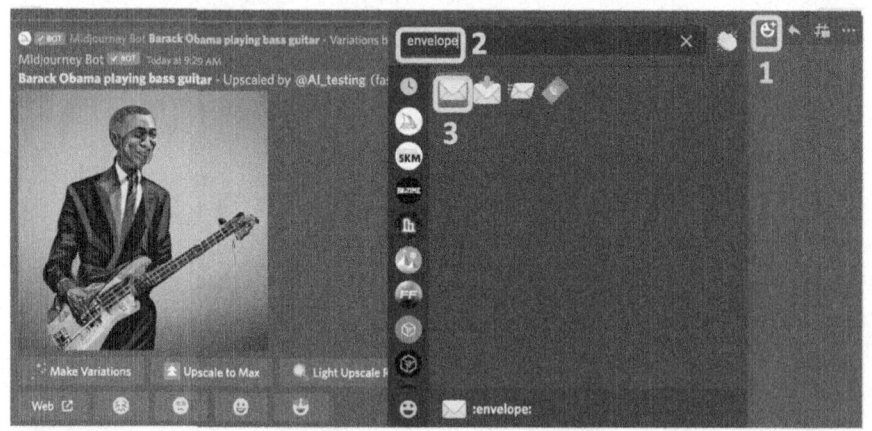

Figure 29: Sending your results as a direct message using the envelope emoji inside Discord

In Figure 29, we can see the final image result in a direct message, which you can find on the left side of the Discord application.

To open the image to full size, simply click on the image. You can also click on "**Open original**" to open the image in your web browser. To save, right-click and choose "**Save image**" from the dropdown menu to save the image to your computer. Note that if you are using Midjourney on the Discord mobile app, you will need to tap the image and then tap on the download icon.

48

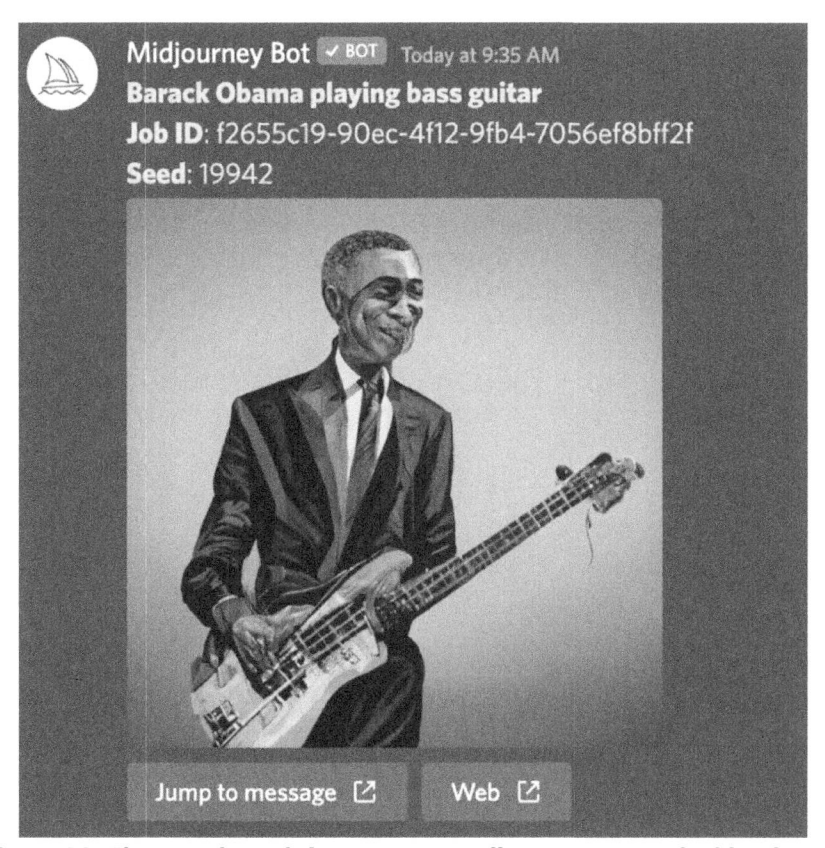

Figure 30: The saved result is sent to your direct messages inside Discord

Other Features

Private and Public Mode
Using **/private** and **/public** you can toggle between private and public mode. In private mode, your jobs are only visible to you. In public mode, your jobs are visible to everyone in the gallery, even if you are creating them in a thread or a direct message.

Show
Using **/show** and inserting the job number, you can recover the ID of a job in your gallery within Discord, displaying the relevant image and the upscale and variation

buttons. This allows you to revive previous jobs and bring them into any Midjourney channel—even if you lose access to the original prompt.

To locate the job number of your art, you must first use the envelope emoji to send the image and metadata (including the job and seed number) as a direct message from Midjourney, which will appear in your chats tab on the left-hand side.

7

AI-GENERATED PROMPTS

In this chapter, we will explore how to take your AI art to the next level by utilizing external AI software to craft text prompts that support your creative vision. By using tools such as Character.ai, you can quickly generate high-quality text-to-image prompts through a user-friendly chat interface.

Character.ai is a software tool that lets you create AI characters that you can chat with, including Elon Musk, Plato, Giga Chad, and even an AI character for teaching you Japanese.

Figure 31: character.ai chat channels

To get started, sign up for a free account, search for the "Midjourney Prompts" character on the platform, and enter a sentence or phrase to outline your artistic vision in the chat box window. Character.ai will then use artificial

51

intelligence to generate image text prompts based on the description you entered, prompts other people are using, as well as all the tutorials it can find online for making images using Midjourney.

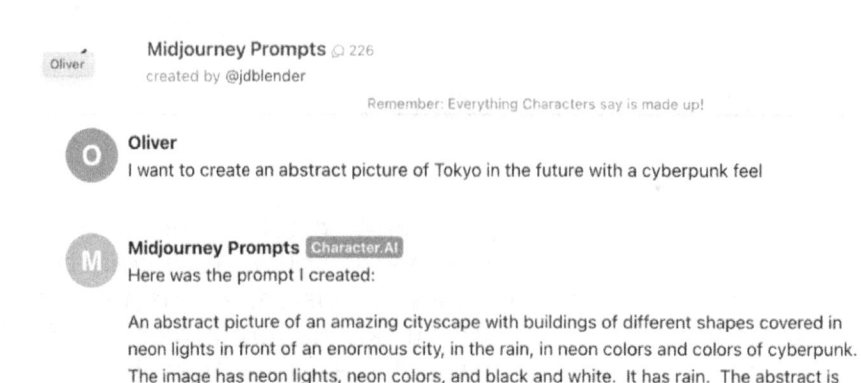

> **Midjourney Prompts** 226
> created by @jdblender
>
> Remember: Everything Characters say is made up!
>
> **Oliver**
> I want to create an abstract picture of Tokyo in the future with a cyberpunk feel
>
> **Midjourney Prompts** Character.AI
> Here was the prompt I created:
>
> An abstract picture of an amazing cityscape with buildings of different shapes covered in neon lights in front of an enormous city, in the rain, in neon colors and colors of cyberpunk. The image has neon lights, neon colors, and black and white. It has rain. The abstract is very detailed and very beautiful.

Figure 32: Using character.ai to create AI-optimized text prompts

You can use these AI-optimized prompts with other AI software or find another character on the platform that supports prompts for your chosen software (i.e. DALL-E or Stable Diffusion). Alternatively, you might like to try ChatGPT (chat.openai.com), created by OpenAI, which is another AI chat tool for generating human-like responses to questions. This can be achieved by providing ChatGPT with some initial text or a basic prompt, and then asking it to generate additional text based on that initial input.

> Create text prompt for DALL-E to create stunning futuristic art with an unusual twist
>
> Create a futuristic art piece depicting a cityscape, but instead of traditional skyscrapers, the buildings are giant mushrooms. The city is bustling with activity and advanced technology, but the mushrooms add an eerie and otherworldly twist.

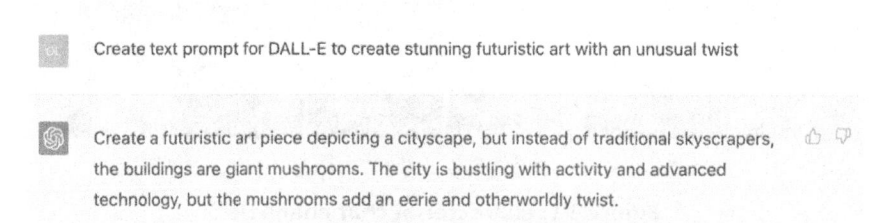

Figure 33: Using ChatGPT to create a text prompt for DALL-E

In Figure 33, I asked ChatGPT to **Create text prompt for DALL-E to create stunning futuristic art with an unusual twist**. Using ChatGPT's answer, I then applied that prompt using DALL-E to generate the results displayed in Figure 34.

Figure 34: DALL-E image results using the text prompt generated by ChatGPT

If you want Midjourney to follow a particular recipe for generating text prompts, you can create a formula and then ask ChatGPT to generate text prompts using that formula.

ChatGPT Prompt 1

DALL-E Prompt Formula:
A highly realistic image of [subject] [doing something interesting] during [time of day] in the style of [artistic style], taken with a [a type of camera], using [type of lens] with [type of lighting]. Do you understand?

ChatGPT Prompt 2

Use formula to create image of a lost temple

Use formula to create image of a lost temple

Certainly! Here's an example of an image generated using the DALL-E 2 prompt formula you provided:

"A highly realistic image of a lost temple surrounded by lush jungle foliage, during the early morning light, in the style of ancient Mayan art, taken with a vintage film camera, using a wide-angle lens with natural lighting filtering through the trees."

Figure 35: ChatGPT's suggested text prompt using a DALL-E 2 formula

53

However, keep in mind that using ChatGPT to generate text-to-image prompts may pose a challenge when working with art software following a new software upgrade, as the new software version may introduce new features or parameters that ChatGPT has not been trained on and is therefore not familiar with.

One effective solution to bridge the knowledge gap is to manually train ChatGPT and teach it about the new software release. By training ChatGPT on the specific features and parameters of the new software version, it can then generate text prompts that are optimized for the software's new capabilities. To train ChatGPT, you can simply copy and paste information related to the new software update into the chat.

For instance, if you wish to use Midjourney's Version 6, which was launched in early 2024, you can visit the official Midjourney documentation (https://docs.midjourney.com/docs/models) and copy relevant information about the new version and paste it into the chat, including any updated parameters and commands. Alternatively, you can copy information about Midjourney V6 from Medium or online blogs and use that as additional training material.

After providing this information, you can ask ChatGPT if it comprehends what Midjourney V6 is, to which it should respond positively. Once you are satisfied with its knowledge of Midjourney V6, you can ask ChatGPT to create a text prompt based on the new software version.

Lastly, for advanced text prompt generation, I recommend using DSNR, which is a Discord-based tool for generating professional image prompts. The tool uses natural language processing and machine learning techniques to analyze your input and generate unique and specific prompts based on your requirements. This tool is useful for product designers wishing to generate images of a product with custom-made features.

To use DSNR, you will need to add the free tool on Discord by navigating to www.discord.gg/SkXXzABWfe. After adding DSNR to Discord, you can navigate to the

"**General**" channel and type **/design** into the chat box. The tool will ask you to specify the style (custom, photorealistic, logo) as well as the subject matter that you wish to create, such as a car, triathlon bike, or watch. Next, the tool will provide a series of prompts to help you generate a customized image prompt that fits your preferences and requirements.

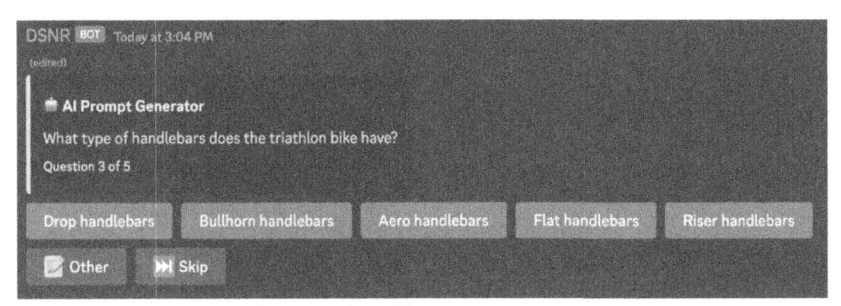

Figure 36: Using the DSNR tool in Discord to generate a text prompt for a custom-made triathlon bike

After completing the prompts, DSNR will generate a text prompt that you can copy and paste into your chosen AI art software.

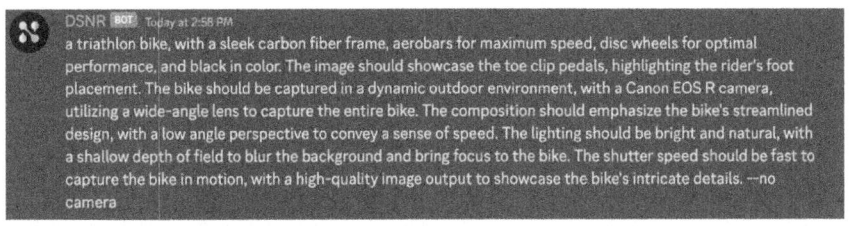

Figure 37: Text prompt for a custom-made triathlon bike generated by DSNR

Using the text prompt provided by DSNR (presented in Figure 37), I was able to generate the following results using Midjourney.

Figure 38: Custom-made triathlon bike using the text prompt generated by DSNR (Midjourney)

8

IMAGE PROMPTS & MASKING

In Chapter 3, we looked at how to create an effective text prompt, but with many AI art software options, it's also possible to incorporate images as part of the prompt. This approach is useful when you want to riff on an existing image or align the output with a particular style. However, it's essential to remember that the AI won't use your image input as a base layer to edit or photoshop it. Although you can adjust the image weighting parameter to help the model capture the visuals of the input image(s), the image is used as a prompt, not as a canvas to edit.

If you wish to upload and edit an existing image, DALL-E lets you do this via a different technique, which we will cover later in this chapter. For now, let's look at how to use images as a prompt with Midjourney.

Demonstration

Within Midjourney, you can upload one or more image URLs and include them in your prompt, which Midjourney will then use as visual inspiration. You can also mix words with images or just use a standalone image as your prompt.

To use an image as a prompt, you will need to navigate to one of the newbies groups inside the Midjourney Discord server. Next, click on the plus icon in the text box (bottom left) and select the first option (**"Upload a File"**).

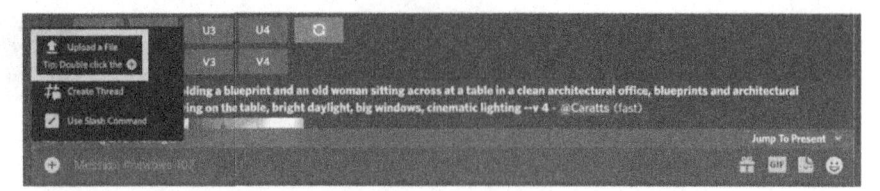

Figure 39: Using Midjourney's Upload a File feature within Discord

Select a file from your computer or album. Here, I'm going to select a Chewbacca puppy image I created using Craiyon.com.

Next, send by hitting Enter on your keyboard. If you scroll down to the bottom of the chat feed, you should find the image you just sent. If you click on the image to enlarge it, you can then right-click on it and select the third menu option called "**Copy Link**".

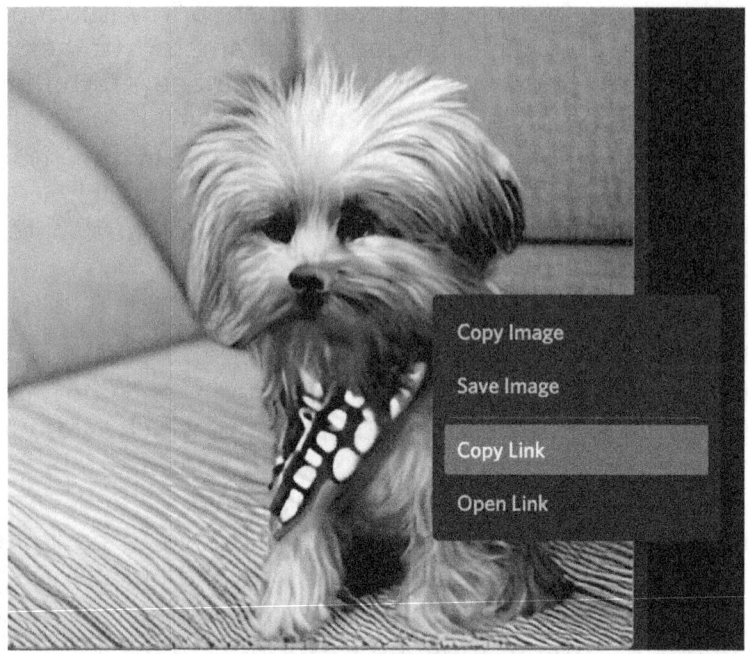

Figure 40: Right-click on the image inside Discord and select the third menu option "Copy Link"

After copying the image, we can get to work with crafting a new text prompt. Let's start by using the **/imagine** command and pasting in the URL link of the image that we just copied. Be sure to leave a space after the URL; using a comma after the URL will corrupt the link.

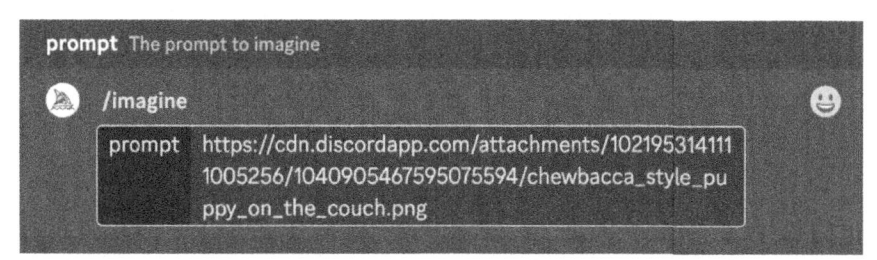

Figure 41: Inserting an image link into a Midjourney text prompt

After adding the image link, you can start defining your prompt, including any modifiers and parameters. For this example, let's add the text prompt: **Chewbacca dog Christmas theme.**

Figure 42: Full text prompt

After sending the image request, Midjourney generated the following image results.

Figure 43: Midjourney image results

We can see that the first and third results capture the Christmas theme. However, the first result in the top-left doesn't look accurate in terms of facial composition.

Let's now riff further on the third result with the Santa cap by clicking on the **V3** button.

Figure 44: Midjourney image variation results for image 3

Based on the results presented in Figure 44, the consistency between the generated results and the uploaded image prompt is still not satisfactory.

It's important to know that the default weighting of the image to the text prompt is 0.25, which means that by default, the text prompt will have a greater impact on the output than the image you used as part of your prompt.

We can adjust the weighting and default settings by adding the parameter **--iw** and inserting the relevant value. For instance, by using the parameter **--iw 1**, you can give equal importance to both your text prompt and the image URL you provide for generating the image. If you want to increase the weighting of the image, then you can push up the weight to 1.5 or higher. Alternatively, you might like to try removing the text prompt altogether and using the image as your only input.

Let's start over again using the same image URL and the same keywords as before, but this time let's add the parameter **--iw 1** to give the image a higher weighting and influence on the image result.

Figure 45: Midjourney image results using a higher image weighting

After modifying the image weighting parameter to give the image prompt greater importance, the generated Chewbacca puppy image looks cuter and more closely resembles the uploaded image prompt. The puppy now has a more contemplative expression, creating a different vibe compared to the original results obtained with the default image weighting value of 0.25. However, the trade-off of this modification is that the image component of the prompt is heavily weighted, causing the keyword **Christmas theme** to be almost completely overridden. This example helps to underline the trade-off that comes with modifying the image weighting parameter.

Lastly, please be careful what images you upload to Discord as it is a public chat tool!

Image Masking

In this next section, we'll delve into a more advanced technique for creating AI art: image masking. While it may seem complex, image masking is straightforward once you understand the process. As part of a demonstration, we'll be using the DALL-E software to showcase this technique.

Demonstration

One of DALL-E's stand-out features is its image uploader. Few AI art software providers currently offer this tool, and in the case of Midjourney, their image uploader is used for supplying image prompts (as a form of inspiration) and not for direct image editing and manipulation. DALL-E, on the other hand, lets you create remixes of an uploaded image or edit the image directly using a technique called masking.

Masking is a technique used in image editing that allows you to select specific parts of an image and then alter that area without affecting the rest of the image. This flexibility makes it ideal for making major alterations to images without drastically changing the overall appearance. Masking is commonly used for removing backgrounds from photos but can also be used to create special effects or isolate certain elements.

In the following demonstration I will show you how to take an existing image, modify it, and add a new background.

Demonstration

After signing up for a DALL-E account, you can use one of your free or paid credits to upload an image via the "**Upload**" button on the right, select an image from your computer, and crop the selected area (if necessary) using the built-in image editor.

Figure 46: DALL-E image generator tool

From there, you should have two choices: 1) "**Edit image**", and 2) "**Generate variations**".

Figure 47: Pick an action > Edit image or Generate variations

Selecting the second option (**Generate variations**) will generate four variations based on the original image (see Figure 48 for example), while clicking on the first option (**Edit image**) will let you directly edit the image using the masking tool.

64

Figure 48: Variations based on the original image on the left. The results on the right look a lot like my real-life brother.

Click on the first option (**Edit image**) and then use the masking wand to erase the area you wish to customize. Don't worry too much about smoothing out the edges. The AI will rebuild the image to protect the edges of the subject or scene, it simply needs a general idea of where to apply the text prompt.

Figure 49: Original image on the left, erased area on the right

Once the desired area for editing has been erased, you can enter your text prompt and click the "**Generate**" button, which will apply to the erased area while also factoring in the style of the non-erased area (that will remain mostly unchanged). Keep in mind that each prompt you submit by clicking the "**Generate**" button will deduct one credit from your account's balance.

Also note that the text prompt should still reference both the area you are modifying and the area you are keeping. As an example, I've uploaded a younger image of myself and used the text prompt **Guy with six pack abs holding**

65

two ice creams after applying image masking to erase the upper part of my torso.

After clicking "**Generate**"**,** DALL-E generated the following output.

Figure 50: Results based on text prompt "Guy with six pack abs holding two ice creams"

While DALL-E didn't fully deliver on the abdominal definition that I had in mind, the generated image is still a significant improvement from the original. DALL-E also did a great job of recreating my skin tone, reconstructing my right arm to hold the second ice cream, as well as touching up my biceps to make them look more defined. It has even extended the image below my waist and provided me with a new pair of black trunks, which seems to be more than what the gentleman on the left is wearing.

You will notice that other elements of the background have changed too. I wish it didn't do that, but it reiterates the importance of linking your text prompt to reflect the entire image and not just the erased area. If you're not satisfied with the generated output, simply click the arrow below the image to view several alternative versions.

After accepting the optimized image, we can use masking again to alter the background. DALL-E's Editor Guide recommends editing the background or scenery last and focusing on the primary subject/character first. In the case of a human subject, this helps to get the body morphology right (which is the more difficult part) before filling in a new background.[2]

Given the current background is not located directly on the beach, I will ask DALL-E to add a new background with the beach behind me. Using the new text prompt: **Guy with six pack abs holding two ice creams on the beach,** I received the following result on the right.

Figure 51: Image result based on text prompt "Guy with six pack abs holding two ice creams on the beach"

The final result isn't perfect—with the background not as photo-realistic as it should be—but with enough credits, you can continue to modify your text prompt and apply image variations until you achieve the desired outcome.

Finally, feel free to experiment with your own images and creative vision to explore the potential of this simple but powerful technique.

---

[2] DALL·E Editor Guide, OpenAI, https://help.openai.com/en/articles/6516417-dall-e-editor-guide, accessed January 16, 2023.

9

FRAMING & LIGHTING

Mastering framing and lighting is essential for crafting art that stands out, giving purpose and context to your designs. Through adept framing and lighting, you can create an atmosphere that enhances the overall message or narrative of your work.

Framing influences how an artwork is composed and presented to your audience. This might include the use of a higher or lower angle, varying depths, and other techniques to create a point of view that guides the viewer's interpretation. Moreover, framing provides visual cues that guide viewers through your creation, while lighting creates depth and contrast to draw attention to specific elements.

Framing

Framing is an essential technique that can take your artwork or photography to the next level. In fact, it is one of the key differentiators between a novice and an advanced user. While beginners tend to focus on the subject matter and adjectives for describing the scene, advanced users understand the importance of the field of view, angle, and the audience's perspective in creating an engaging and meaningful piece of art. By carefully choosing the framing of your artwork, you can create a sense of depth, intimacy, or grandeur, and direct the viewer's attention to the most important elements of your work. If you have any experience in TV and film, framing will come naturally to you. If not, it's a relatively easy skill to learn. Once you become more acquainted, you will start to notice how these techniques are used in the media or your favorite Netflix show to add dramatic effect.

There are no strict rules for framing, only possibilities to explore, which makes framing an exciting technique for experimentation. Artists, for example, might emphasize certain aspects of their subject matter while de-emphasizing others. Common examples include using a low angle to make a subject look more powerful or using a deeper focus to give more space around the subject and draw attention to its details. Framing also allows you to create illusions in your artwork such as making objects appear larger or smaller than they are.

Specific examples of framing include point-of-view (POV), wide-shot, over-the-shoulder, front-on, long-shot, and close-up shot. Below is a list of some common framing angles used in photography, film, and art using image examples generated by Stable Diffusion.

Over-the-shoulder

This type of shot is a great way to capture two people in conversation. It can be used to create tension and suspense by focusing on one subject while the other isn't fully shown.

Extreme Close-Up

This frame is usually used to intensify emotions, such as fear or excitement. It can be especially effective when you want to get your audience into the character's headspace.

Wide Shot

A wide shot is used to show all the characters or subjects in the scene and their respective interactions. It provides a sense of scale and can be used to establish a location or environment.

Dutch Angle

The Dutch angle is designed to unsettle the viewer by tilting the angle off-axis. It's often used to create an atmosphere of unease, disorientation, or confusion.

High Angle Shot

A high angle shot is usually taken from above a character's head in order to make them look more smaller or powerless than they actually are. It's often used to emphasize the power dynamics in a scene and create tension.

Isometric

Isometric is a method for visually representing 3D objects in 2D, and is often used in technical and engineering drawings, such as town planning documents.

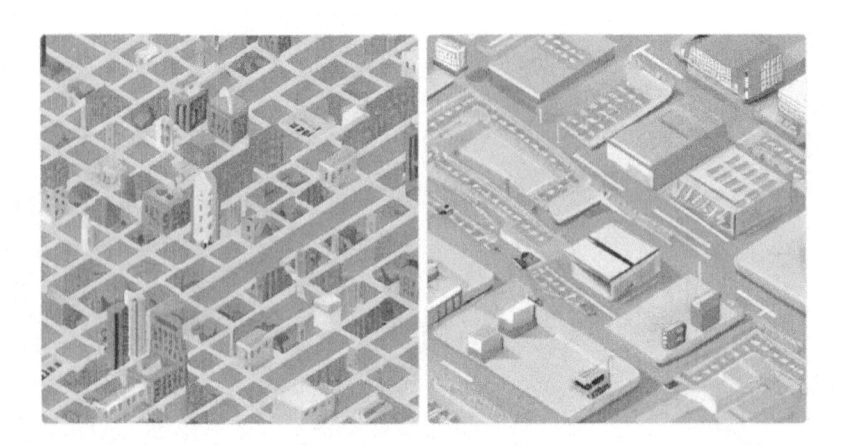

By understanding the principles and different styles behind framing and perspective, you will be able to create more impactful art that captures your audience's attention and evokes an emotional response. Generating an image of someone making a speech to a room full of people will yield different results depending on the point of view, for instance.

Figure 52: A person making a speech from an over-the-shoulder angle (Stable Diffusion)

Figure 53: A person making a speech from the audience's point of view (Stable Diffusion)

Likewise, framing the view of a city from an isometric perspective (representing 3D objects in 2D) will provide a drastically different view than if you used a plain text prompt with no specific framing information.

If you're looking for more knowledge and inspiration regarding framing, you might like to check out www.nfi.edu/types-of-film-shots, which documents 80+ different framing angles, including the cowboy shot (shows the subject from the mid-thigh and up).

Lighting

More subtle than framing, lighting is useful for making a scene look more polished and for highlighting certain features or characters. By understanding lighting and using it to your advantage, you can make art that truly stands out and leaves a lasting impression on your audience.

Below is a list of some of the most popular lighting techniques used by filmmakers and artists that you can incorporate into your text prompts. Image examples are again generated using Stable Diffusion.

Three-Point Lighting

This technique involves using three lights in order to achieve an even balance between light and shadow on the subject's face. It typically consists of two side lights (or key lights) and one backlight (or fill light). The key lights provide illumination on either side of the subject while the fill light softens shadows caused by the key lights and adds depth to the composition.

Backlighting

This technique involves lighting the subject from behind in order to create a halo effect or silhouette. It's great for creating depth and drawing attention to certain elements of the scene.

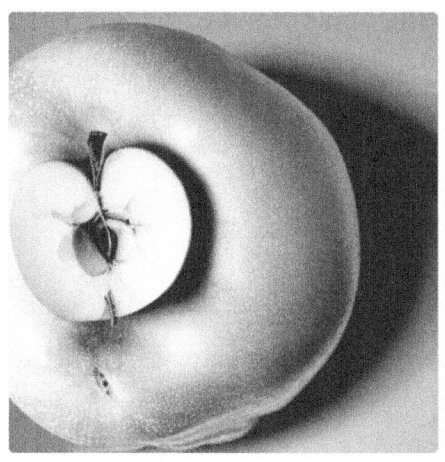

High-Key Lighting

This technique is used for bright, cheerful scenes that don't have any shadows or dark tones. The key light (the main source of illumination) should be placed at a high angle so that it creates soft shadows, and there may also be additional fill lights to add extra light to the scene.

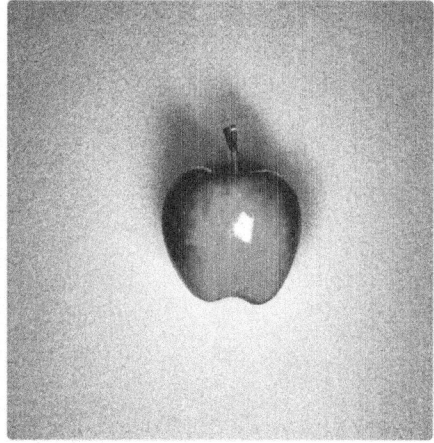

Low-Key Lighting

This technique is used for dramatic scenes with lots of shadows and darker tones. The key light should be placed low and off to one side so that it creates deep shadows, and there may be additional fill lights to add light to the scene as well.

Rembrandt Lighting

This technique is named after the Dutch painter who used it frequently in his paintings. It's often used for portraitures and consists of a key light placed slightly off center, with a triangle of light visible under one eye and cheekbone.

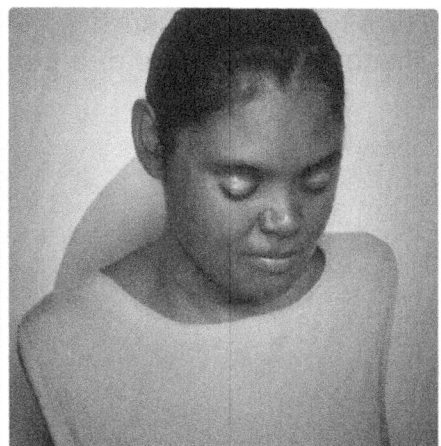

Butterfly Lighting

This technique involves placing a key light directly above the subject, creating a butterfly-shaped shadow on their nose and chin. It's great for emphasizing facial features like eyes or strong jawlines.

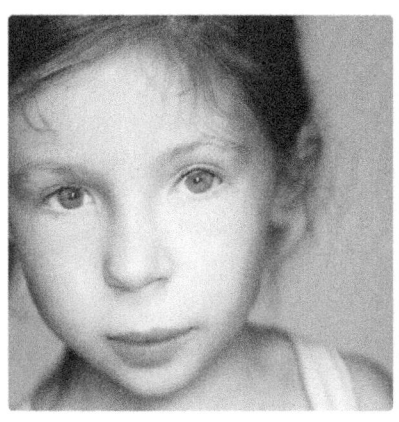

Soft Lighting

Soft lighting is often used to create mood and atmosphere. It involves diffusing light by bouncing it off other surfaces or using modifiers like umbrellas and softboxes. Soft lighting produces low contrast, which can be useful in certain situations, such as when you want to reduce harsh shadows on the face of a portrait subject.

10

PARAMETERS

Now that you're more familiar with using text prompts and a variety of modifiers including framing and lighting, let's talk about advanced commands using what are called "parameters", "switches", or "flags".

Note that parameters, including how they are triggered and defined, are subject to the software solution you are using. This means you will need to familiarize yourself with the unique parameters for each software solution you wish to use. Also, in some cases, basic software will have few to no parameters available, which means you'll need to look for more advanced options such as Midjourney and DALL-E to unleash your full artistic potential.

For this chapter, we will be using Midjourney to demonstrate different parameter options.

Earlier, in Chapter 6, we learned how to create a basic text prompt in Midjourney using **/imagine** to produce a grid of four images.

Example 1
/imagine battle on a desolate planet, cyberpunk style

To customize the text prompt, we can add parameters using two consecutive dashes "**--**" followed by the parameter we wish to use

Example 2
/imagine battle on a desolate planet, cyberpunk style --no cars

In Example 2, we are using negative prompting by telling the AI to avoid adding cars to the image results. Keep in mind that the parameters should be added at the end of the text prompt rather than at the front or midway through the prompt. Failure to do so may make your jobs partially or completely unusable.

Common Midjourney Parameters

Let's now look at some of the commonly used parameters available with Midjourney.

Negative Prompting

The first common parameter is negative prompting using **--no {keyword}**, which you can use to avoid adding elements to your image. Double-dash no humans, for instance, would try to remove humans from the generation.

Example 3

/imagine Osaka, blade runner, cinematic lighting, slight tilt--no humans, no people

Figure 54: Two image results, with negative prompting on the right

Above are two examples. On the left, we can see one person in the image by default, and on the right, we can see there's a clear absence of people given that we used the parameter **--no humans, no people**.

Size & Dimensions

Next, let's talk about size and dimensions using **aspect** or **ar**. These two parameters allow you to generate images according to your desired aspect ratio. Using **--ar 16:9**, for example, will give you an aspect ratio of 16:9 (or 448 x 256 pixels).

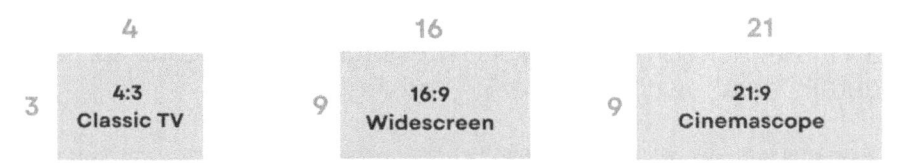

Figure 55: Examples of how the aspect ratio impacts image size

If you wish to match your image with a specific aspect ratio, you can check with the software you are using, and then enter the width and height into the height and width parameters.

Below are two more examples that again show the role of size and dimensions in creating art.

--ar 15:15

--ar 18:9

Figure 56: Two more different aspect ratios using Midjourney

Seeds

Seed numbers are used for reproducing art using the same randomization used to generate the original version. Using the same seed number will help you recreate a similar output using the same prompt.

A seed number must be a positive integer (any whole number between 0 and 4294967295). If you don't set a seed, a random seed will be assigned instead. To find out what seed was used behind the scenes, you can react with the envelope (✉) emoji to an image (by clicking on the Add Reaction icon on the far right and searching "envelope") and then check your direct messages on Discord for the details as shown in Figure 57 and Figure 58.

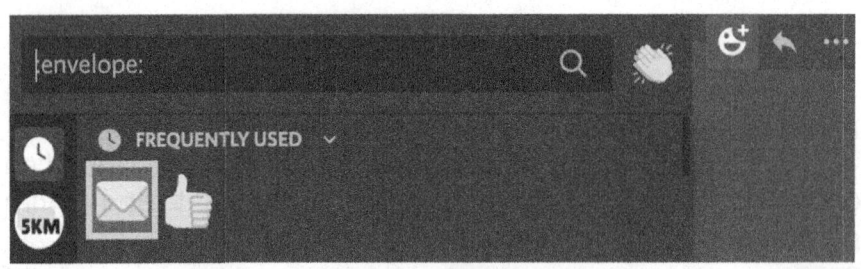

Figure 57: Use the envelope emoji to send your image results as a direct message

Figure 58: Image result and metadata inside Discord Direct Messages

In Figure 58, we can see the Seed is 453857926.

While seeds are an important technique in machine learning and for generating AI art, it is important to note that the seed technique is not perfect and based on my

82

experience so far, I wouldn't expect to see the exact same output (but this feature might get better in the future).

Looking at the results in Figure 59, it's fair to say that the style is similar, but the exact image content is different and by no means a carbon copy.

Figure 59: Image results using the same seed number

Chaos

If you want to want to push the boundaries of your AI creations, then you may like to test the parameter **--chaos {num}**, which introduces more varied, random, and different image results. The number used with this parameter must be between 0 and 100. Higher values will favor more extreme and unusual generations in exchange for less reliable compositions.

Example 4

/imagine Osaka, blade runner, cinematic lighting, slight tilt—chaos 70

Figure 60: Image results using the chaos parameter (--chaos 70)

In Figure 60, I used the same text prompt as I used in previous examples but with a high chaos number of **70** which generated some unique and unexpected results.

Video

Using the parameter **--video**, you can save the progress of your image generation as a moving image, which captures the iterative production of your image generation as a video. The video link is sent to you after you use the envelope (✉) emoji in Discord to trigger a direct message.

Quality Values

Image quality is vital when it comes to AI art and using the quality modifier in Midjourney will offer you more control over what resources are consumed generating your image. At present, there are five image quality options as follows:

Parameter	Quality	Efficiency	Note
--quality 0.25	Rough	4x faster/cheaper	
--quality 0.5	Less detailed	2x faster/cheaper	
--quality 1	Default value	Standard/default	No need to define
--quality 2	More detailed	2x slower & 2x the price	Higher GPU usage (2 GPUs)
--quality 5	More experimental/ creative/risky	Slow & expensive	Very high GPU usage (5 GPUs)

Table 1: Midjourney image quality parameters

By default, you will mostly be using the default value which is 1 and does not need to be specified in your text prompts. However, if you are looking for higher or lower quality results you can use one of the other four options to tune the output quality of your image generation.

To learn more, check out Midjourney's documentation at https://docs.midjourney.com and note that some of these parameters may be tweaked or deprecated in the future. The **beta** and **hq** algorithm parameters, for example, have already been discontinued at the time of writing. Likewise, new parameters will be introduced over time, so always keep an eye out for new advanced settings.

CONSISTENCY

From comics and books to films and storyboards, the ability to create consistent and recognizable characters is a crucial part of producing visual media. However, this can be a challenge when working with generative AI art. Due to the complex nature of AI models, the images generated by algorithms are inherently unique and they can vary greatly from one generation to the next. This can be beneficial for creating unique images, but it can be a problem when trying to maintain a consistent representation of a character across multiple different scenes and situations.

Uploading images of an existing subject as part of your prompt with the intention of replicating it may seem like an obvious approach, but it's not always guaranteed to deliver the desired outcome. Even with the use of a seed number, which few AI software solutions (excluding Midjourney) currently offer, the results are not guaranteed (seed numbers are designed for replicating the same image and not the same character across different scenes). The difficulty in achieving character consistency lies in the fact that AI art models have a bias toward creating new variations and are not designed to maintain consistency.

As a result, the AI art community is highly active in exploring alternative techniques and workarounds to achieve character consistency. From using famous people as an anchor point to handpicking characters from a massive collection of images, there are many methods for improving artistic consistency. In this chapter, we will explore several character consistency techniques including the challenges and limitations of each technique.

The Famous Person Approach

One of the easiest ways to create standard characters or environments is to use well-known existing examples as your starting point. By selecting well-known examples as the base of your character or setting, you can create a person or place that is more consistent and recognizable across multiple images.

In the case of a physical setting, this may involve using specific descriptions such as **Shibuya crossing in Tokyo** or **Hogwarts Castle** rather than generic descriptions such as a **Tokyo intersection** and a **British castle**.

For human characters, you can use famous and established celebrities as a starting point. This approach has been popularized by artists such as Kris Kashtanova, who created the first AI-generated graphic novel, *Zarya of the Dawn*.

Figure 61: *Zarya Of the Dawn* by Kristina Kashtanova

In her work, Kris chose to use the American actress Zendaya as the base of her main character. By using Zendaya in her text prompts, Kris was able to leverage the AI's existing knowledge of the American actress's appearance, personality, and mannerisms to create a character that was consistent and recognizable across multiple images.

Another advantage of using famous examples as your starting point is that it streamlines the creative process. By starting with a well-known example, you don't have to spend time and effort defining the character's physical appearance and personality. Instead, you can focus on creating the story and generating images of the character across different scenarios and environments.

Having discussed the benefits of using famous people as a standard character, let's test this technique using Ryan Reynolds as the base of a new character. In this example, we will create a 35-year-old medieval king using the Hollywood actor Ryan Reynolds as a starting point. To do this, let's enter the following text prompt inside Midjourney.

Example
/imagine Ryan Reynolds as a 35-year-old medieval king, 8k

Figure 62: Ryan Reynolds as a 35-year-old medieval king, 8k

Using Ryan as an anchor point allows us to leverage the existing recognition and familiarity of the Hollywood actor to create a consistent and recognizable character for our content. In fact, from the output Midjourney has given us, we could use three of the four variations (excluding the bottom-left result) given there is a consistent resemblance between these three images.

However, it's important to note that there are clear drawbacks to using famous people in your art. First, you may need to obtain permission from the person or their representatives to use their image and likeness in your work. Second, relying too heavily on a well-known public figure as the basis for your character limits creativity and makes it difficult to differentiate your work from others or differentiate your character from people's existing knowledge of that person.

Fortunately, there is a path around this problem. AI art enthusiasts active on Reddit have discovered that by swapping certain characteristics, such as the race and sex of a famous person, they can minimize or overcome some of the limitations mentioned. By swapping out characteristics, the character becomes a unique and original creation, rather than a direct representation of a famous person. Using this technique, artists can therefore create a consistent and recognizable character while still maintaining their own creative vision and avoiding potential legal issues.

Let's try this technique using Paris Hilton in place of Ryan Reynolds as the seed for our medieval king.

Example 1

/imagine Paris Hilton as a 35-year-old male medieval king, 8k

You may also like to use negative prompting to reduce the likelihood of the model producing a female character.

Example 2

/imagine Paris Hilton as a 35 year-old male medieval king, 8k, --no female, woman

Figure 63: Paris Hilton as a 35-year-old male medieval king, 8k --no female, woman

The image results are not as consistent as the Ryan Reynolds version, but we can see some consistent facial elements, such as the long narrow nose and blue eyes. Also, the goal here isn't to produce four versions that closely resemble each other but rather to find a text prompt that we can use in the future for inserting our character into new scenes and situations.

The More Detailed Approach
The next trick to improve consistency is to add more details. By simply adding more details to your text prompt, you can improve the results significantly. By adding physical details such as ethnicity, haircut, hair color, eyes, and face structure to the text prompt as well as stylistic details,

including lighting and camera angle, we can narrow down the range of potential variations and maintain overall consistency.

Example 2

/imagine Paris Hilton as a 35-year-old male medieval king looking straight into the camera in the style of a marvel comic, anglo-saxon, neck-length blonde hair, blue eyes, angular face structure, 8k --no female, women

Figure 64: Paris Hilton as a 35-year-old male medieval king looking straight into the camera in the style of a marvel comic, anglo-saxon, neck-length blonde hair, blue eyes, angular face structure, 8k --no female, women

In some scenarios, your attempts at replicating an existing character or scene using AI art software may not produce the desired outcome. If this occurs, you may need to go back and analyze the original version to determine what qualities are missing. For instance, you may find that the original character has a different skin complexion, reflecting an almost German or Asian-looking appearance. By analyzing the original version and identifying these details, you can then revisit your text prompt and insert those missing characteristics. This will help to ensure that the AI model generates images of the character that are consistent with the original version.

The Some of Many Versions Approach

Another popular technique is to mass-produce your target output before hand-selecting images that closely match or that maintain some level of consistency. According to successful record producer, Rick Rubin, the best way to create hit records (or make something that is great) is: "If you need 10 of something, make 30. Then pick the best." This principle certainly applies to AI art, where multiple attempts are needed in order to find and curate the best possible versions.

However, in the case of some paid software tools, this approach will quickly consume your credits, with each credit producing 4-6 images. To conserve resources, you may want to switch to using Stable Diffusion or another free software service that allows you to create unlimited images. I prefer to use Stable Diffusion as it supports negative prompting, which is useful if you want to swap the gender or ethnicity of a famous person (as we did in the previous example).

The Contact Sheet Approach

The next effective technique to improve consistency is to add the terms **multiple poses and expressions** and/or **contact sheet** to your prompt. This will help to generate something similar to a contact sheet, which is typically used by photographers and designers to review photos or graphics from a selection of images arranged on a single sheet of paper.

Example
/imagine cute owl in multiple poses and expressions

Using several contact sheets, you can then export the results to Photoshop or your chosen image editing software and isolate each version of the character from the original background. This way, you create a database of images that you can use to maintain character consistency in your work.

Next, you may need to upscale and enhance the file size of the original output by using a free service such as Upscale Media (www.upscale.media) or an upscale feature that comes built-in with the software. Increasing the resolution and file size of your images can help offset the sacrifice in image quality that occurs from creating a contact sheet with multiple versions of a subject contained inside a limited space. Alternatively, you could increase the image aspect ratio of the image in order to provide a larger canvas.

Figure 65: Cute owl in multiple poses and expressions

The Alternative Angle Approach

As a final stopgap solution, you can try creating images of your subject from different angles or perspectives. For example, you might create images of the character located further away from the camera or standing with their back to the camera to fill scenes where a close-up and front-on version of the character are not needed.

This technique can be especially useful in scenes where the character is not the primary focus, or where the emphasis is on the setting or background rather than the character. Most importantly, it saves you spending an inordinate amount of time recreating the character for every scene.

12

REMIXING POPULAR STYLES OF ART

When it comes to artistic expression, there are almost as many styles as there are works of art.

There's no right or wrong approach, so don't be afraid to experiment. Exploring different styles will give you a better understanding of art and help you develop your own unique style. With practice, you may even come up with a new style.

To help you explore the different range of artistic styles available, I have included a list of popular styles and artists, as well as some sample text prompts.

The sample images included in this chapter were generated using DALL-E, using the first sample prompt listed in each section.

Impressionism

This style focuses on capturing a moment in time with loose brush strokes and vibrant colors. Think Monet or Cassatt for examples of this type of art.

Sample prompts

1. A sunlit garden in full bloom, captured in a flurry of vibrant brushstrokes, impressionist style
2. An impressionist painting of a peaceful lakeside scene, rendered in soft hazy tones, Monet style
3. A romantic stroll through a park, captured in an impressionistic style

4. A lively part scene, painted with swirling colors and a sense of movement in the style of impressionism and Cassatt
5. A foggy morning on the river, rendered in soft, misty impressionist hues

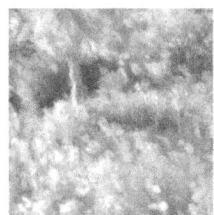

Expressionism

Artists who choose expressionism focus on conveying emotion through distorted forms, intense colors, and exaggerated lines. Some well-known expressionists include Munch and Schiele.

Sample prompts

1. Paint a scene that represents the chaos and confusion of modern society in the style of expressionism
2. Depict the feeling of being trapped in your own mind through a collage, expressionist art in the style of Munch
3. Express the beauty in imperfection through a sculpture using expressionist techniques
4. Create a digital piece that illustrates the power of the subconscious in the style of expressionism
5. Design a mural that represents the struggle for self-acceptance in the style of Schiele

Realism

This style seeks to depict life as it is, with an emphasis on detail and accuracy. Millet, Courbet, and Daumier fall into this category. To achieve this style of art, you may need to add more details to the text prompt to capture the scene you wish to compose.

Sample prompts

1. Capture this moment in a realistic painting: a cityscape at sunset, with the warm orange glow illuminating the tall skyscrapers and busy streets. The hustle and bustle of the city are palpable, as people hurry to and fro.
2. Convey the emotions and atmosphere of the following scene in a realistic drawing: A lone figure sits on a park bench, lost in thought. The autumn leaves falling around them add to the sense of solitude and introspection. Style of Courbet.
3. Create a realistic painting that captures the tranquillity of a fisherman standing on the edge of a pier, casting his lines into the calm waters below. The early morning mist also creates a serene and peaceful atmosphere.
4. Create a realistic painting that captures the energy and life of a busy market with people haggling and bargaining for the best deals. Use vibrant colors to convey the energy of the busy market. Style of Millet.
5. An old, abandoned factory stands in the middle of a field. The rusting metal and crumbling concrete are a stark contrast to the lush greenery around it. Create a realistic painting that captures the eerie beauty and decay of this abandoned industrial site.

Abstract

The goal of abstract art is to evoke feelings through composition rather than tangible objects or figures. Rothko and Mondrian are two iconic abstract painters.

Sample prompts

1. Design a world where emotions are represented by abstract shapes and colors
2. Create art that represents the chaos of the modern world through abstract forms and textures in the style of Rothko
3. Visualize the concept of infinity through abstract shapes and lines in the style of abstract art
4. Explore the theme of duality through contrasting abstract shapes and colors
5. Imagine a dreamlike world and depict it through abstract shapes and colors

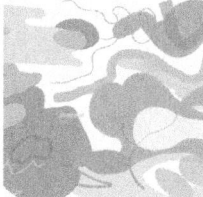

Pop Art

This is my preferred style. In pop art, everyday images like advertisements or comic books are reframed in a way that makes them seem more artistic or interesting. Warhol and Lichtenstein are examples of well-known pop artists.

Sample prompts

1. Create a Pop Art inspired image of a robot uprising
2. Create a Pop Art interpretation of the AI singularity in the style of Warhol
3. Design a Pop Art inspired advertisement for a house cleaning product

4. Create a Pop Art portrait of a Japanese salaryman
5. Pop Art-ify a vision of a world where AI and humans coexist, Lichtenstein style

Surrealism

Surrealists try to express their dreamlike visions by combining elements from reality with the unreal. Salvador Dali and Magritte are two of the most famous surrealists.

Sample prompts

1. Design a world where giant robots roam the desert, surrounded by floating cities and twisted, abstract landscapes, Surrealist style
2. Picture a surreal landscape where the sky is made of swirling, psychedelic colors and the ground is covered in a lush, overgrown jungle
3. Create a city where the buildings are made of clouds, and the streets are filled with giant, sentient flowers in the style of Salvador Dali
4. The world is a giant, living organism, and every person and thing is a tiny part of its intricate, pulsating system
5. Design a surreal landscape where the laws of physics don't apply, and gravity is inverted, making everything float and spin in unexpected ways

Contemporary Art

This style is more focused on the ideas and concepts behind the artwork, rather than its form or aesthetics. It's constantly evolving as the world changes and new forms of expression are explored. Koons and Hirst are two great examples of contemporary artists. You will almost definitely need to add **contemporary art** to the text prompt to capture this artistic style.

Sample prompts

1. Depict a new world where machines create art, in the style of contemporary art
2. Create a contemporary art style piece that represents the intersection of technology and nature in the style of Koons
3. Hand-paint a scene that reflects the chaos and beauty of the city in the style of contemporary art
4. Create a photo that represents the tension between the past and the future in the style of contemporary art
5. Contemporary art showing a rapidly changing world and the complexities of human experience

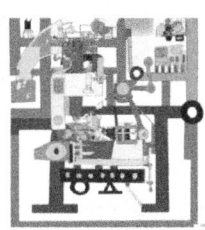

Folk Art

This style is rooted in tradition and the culture of a particular region. It often has a naive quality and can include any form of art from painting to sculpture or weaving. Grandma Moses was one of the most beloved folk artists of all time.

Sample prompts

1. Generate a colorful quilt pattern inspired by traditional folk art motifs
2. Create a digital painting of a whimsical folk art scene featuring animals and nature elements in the style of Grandma Moses
3. Generate a digital print featuring a folk art-inspired abstract design, using bold colors and geometric shapes
4. Design a digital collage of folk art images, featuring a mix of traditional and modern elements
5. Create a digital animation of a folk art-inspired mural, featuring movement and interactive elements

Outsider Art

Outsider art is often created by people without formal training, such as the mentally ill or children. Dubuffet and Basquiat are two popular outsider artists.

Sample prompts

1. Create an abstract portrait of a robot's inner emotions in the style of outsider art
2. Design a surreal landscape depicting a world ruled by AI in the style of Basquiat
3. Illustrate the collision of technology and nature through outsider art
4. Create a mixed media sculpture representing the relationship between humans and animals in the style of outsider art
5. Create a graffiti-style mural depicting the rebellion against government oppression, outsider art

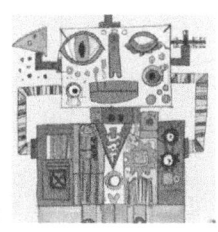

Cubism

This style is characterized by abstract shapes and facets that are combined to create an overall image. Braque and Picasso were two of the most influential cubists.

Sample prompts

1. Transform a classic portrait into a Cubist masterpiece
2. Create a digital collage of geometric shapes in the style of Picasso
3. Generate a Cubist landscape, blending abstract forms with realistic elements
4. Generate a series of Cubist still lifes, blending geometric shapes with organic forms in the style of Braque
5. Create a Cubist cityscape, blending abstract forms with recognizable Paris landmarks

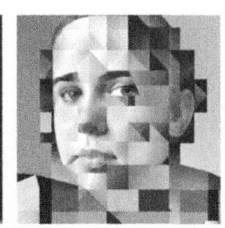

USEFUL TEXT PROMPTS

Below are some useful text prompt templates you can use to experiment as you familiarize yourself with your chosen software. You may also like to check out Lexica Art (lexica.art), which offers a free text prompt library based on images generated using Stable Diffusion, or arthub.ai to explore other images and prompts from top community artists and designers.

At the time of writing, examples of trending prompts include **raw photo**, **multiple exposure photography**, and **trending on artstation**.

a dark glowing forest in _____ and _____ with sky burning

an epic temple in _____ and futuristic _____ suspended in the air

the gloomy gateway to _____ and _____ with luminescent blue dust

the angel of _____ and _____ surrounded in darkness, cinematic lighting

a photorealistic 8k shot of the emperor/empress of _____ with dynamic lighting

a biblical fantasy illustration of _____ with insane detail

high definition and photorealistic view of an ancient _____ painting

Hollywood movie still of _____ and _____ with focused lighting and a slight tilt

a grainy, portrait style photograph of the final _____

a professional photo of _____

neon view of _____ at night

_____ and _____ in a filigree metal design

_____ in the style of a 70s science fiction book cover

_____ in the style of a metal album cover

_____ in the style of cyberpunk noir art deco

_____ in the style of glitch art

_____ in the style of cyberpunk with cinematic lighting

14

IMAGE RIGHTS

Similar to the existence of official licensing terms of service within the stock photography industry, rules and rights govern the domain of AI art. Understanding these rules and rights will help to ensure that any AI-generated artworks you create and sell comply with relevant copyright laws.

Copyright law is a legal framework that grants creators exclusive rights over their original creative works. As a form of intellectual property protected by law in a given jurisdiction, owning the copyright of your artwork gives you the exclusive right to reproduce, publish, or sell that original work. Under copyright laws in the U.S., for example, artists who employ traditional mediums, such as paint, pen, or paper, hold copyright over their work by default. This helps to protect the rights of creators by giving them the authority to control how their works are used, reproduced, distributed, and displayed. This protection is also intended to encourage creativity and provide creators with the opportunity to benefit financially and artistically from their creations.

The copyright considerations for generative AI art, however, are notably complex—as the technology is still relatively new and the legal principles that govern traditional forms of artwork don't always apply. For example, under copyright law set by the U.S. Copyright Office, an author's exclusive right to reproduce their work does not apply if a work has been generated by a computer process that operates randomly or mechanically without any human authorship. This means that if a human did not author the work, the Copyright Office won't register any copyright, leaving the door wide open for public use.

According to Steven Ellison, a lawyer and legal writer, "In the eyes of the Copyright Office, the public is free to reproduce, publish, or sell your DALL-E-generated masterpiece, no strings attached."[3] Ellison suggests that Congress in the U.S. could bypass the Copyright Office in the future to recognize the copyright of generative AI work under the law, but as it stands, there is little copyright protection for AI art in the U.S., at least.[4]

In addition, it's not always clearcut who the sole owner of the AI-generated art should be. In general, copyright belongs to the creator or author of a work (i.e., the person responsible for its creation), but in the case of AI art, this definition could include the programmer and company who designed and developed the large language model and software used to generate the art, the owners of any datasets used to train the model or those with rights to any copyrighted content incorporated into the artwork, and of course, the end-user involved in creative decisions about how that technology was used to produce the final artwork. Each of these stakeholders could be considered an author and therefore entitled to owning the copyright. Therefore, it is important to consider not only who owns the copyright but also who else may need to be consulted and/or given permission before an AI artwork can be sold or shared.

In sum, the copyright considerations for AI art are complex and require careful consideration of who owns rights in the work, as well as how it can be reproduced and distributed. While this is a complex topic, your chosen AI art software provider should serve as the primary point of reference for information regarding copyright and terms of use.

Craiyon, for example, does not allow users to make any unauthorized use of images that may infringe on the intellectual property rights of Craiyon or third parties such

---

[3] Steven Ellison, FindLaw, www.findlaw.com/legalblogs/legally-weird/who-owns-dall-e-images, accessed November 14, 2022.

[4] Steven Ellison, FindLaw, www.findlaw.com/legalblogs/legally-weird/who-owns-dall-e-images, accessed November 14, 2022.

as Disney and FIFA, or conduct commercial activities using art generated on their platform. This means that the content you create on Craiyon should be used solely for personal use and not for commercial purposes—unless you receive written permission from Craiyon and/or a given third-party. In addition, you do not acquire any ownership rights over those images created using Craiyon.

In the case of DALL-E, you must agree to OpenAI's Terms of Use, which assigns OpenAI ownership of the generated images that you create. OpenAI, grants users the right to sell your images; however, as the owner of the image, OpenAI is also able to grant others the right to reproduce, publish, or sell images that you create using their software. In other words, you can commercially use and sell your DALL-E-generated images but there is also nothing stopping others from doing the same using your artwork!

With Midjourney, meanwhile, you own the content assets you create using that service even after your subscription has expired. However, there are two important exceptions to take note of.

First, if you upscale an image of another user, that upscale is owned by the original creator and not you, which means that you will need their permission to use it. Second, owners or employees working at a company generating over USD $1 million in yearly gross revenue and using their services to benefit their employer or company must purchase a Pro or Megan Plan to use images commercially. The Pro plan currently costs USD $576 per year and USD $1,152 for Mega.

At the time of writing, Midjourney offers you more mileage with ownership and non-commercial licensing than DALL-E, Craiyon, and most other AI software solutions. For commercial licensing terms, make sure that you are paying for the service and if you are representing a large company, you will need to invest in a Mega or Pro Plan.

Lastly, note that by using Midjourney's services, you grant Midjourney a worldwide, non-exclusive, royalty-free, irrevocable copyright license to reproduce derivative works based on image prompts or content you feed into their platform. This means that others can remix your images and prompts whenever they are posted in a public setting.

15

ETHICS, PRIVACY & ORIGINALITY

As a new technology, we are still grappling to understand the extent and nature of bias and privacy risks associated with text-to-image models. While we know the capabilities of these models are impressive, it's important to recognize that they could be magnifying and mirroring societal biases on a global scale. With AI art models trained on private datasets or data crawled from the Internet, there's a possibility that they could produce images embodying or purporting harmful stereotypes.

As an example, the project thispersondoesnotexist.com, which generates a hyper-realistic portrait of a person who never existed, has been widely criticized for failing to generate people with black skin color, which alludes to issues with the training data used to create the model. (It's worth noting that the project was spun up as an online stunt and demonstration to build awareness regarding the powerful capabilities of AI rather than as a fully polished software product.)

The next major concern comes with deep fakes, which are digital images or videos that have been manipulated and can be used to deceive people—often for malicious purposes. Deep fakes present a unique problem because they can easily be mistaken for reality and can cause significant damage when used in this way. For example, these technologies can be used to spread false information about individuals or organizations, put public figures in compromising positions, incite protests, or even manipulate elections.

Privacy is another contentious issue, especially as AI models are constantly learning and potentially using your inputs to retrain their model, meaning that some of your art's DNA could potentially go into producing other AI-generated art in ways you never anticipated. If you upload a photo of yourself and tell the AI software to remix that photo in a certain way, both the input (which is the original photo of you) and the output (the remixed version) could be used by the model to retrain its model. In most cases, this is unlikely to have any real effect, unless you are feeding the algorithm significant amounts of input data to train on. However, in some cases, it may be important for the user to protect the privacy of their images. In such cases, it's best to check the platform's terms of service or avoid using such services if you have any concerns.

If you're creating art using Midjourney, be aware that Midjourney is an open community and any image you generate in a public Discord chatroom is viewable by all others in that chatroom. This stands in contrast to other platforms where you interact with the AI on a one-to-one basis, ensuring that only you have access to the outcomes.

Whether it's Midjourney or another software option, you should always be careful with what you feed into the model, especially private images or information you wouldn't want to leak publicly.

Next comes the contentious issue of originality. While each artist differs stylistically, they also consume, learn, and remodel the artistic process of many artists who came before them. Training AI models to produce generated art follows a similar pattern, just far more obvious. While it is certainly possible to create "original" works of art using artificial intelligence, at their core, these models rely on pre-existing datasets of human-generated art. This can be viewed as unoriginal and unethical—especially if remnants of the artist's signature are still visible in the bottom left-hand corner, *which has happened*! Additionally, AI models might be trained to replicate the style of an artist without their knowledge or permission.

To counter this problem, start-ups such as Originality.ai and Detect GPT are creating tools to detect AI-generated content or plagiarism and protect the rights of the original creators. The current technology, however, performs better at identifying GPT-3 and ChatGPT-generated text content rather than AI-generated images.

OpenAI, the creator of ChatGPT and DALL-E, is also developing cryptographic technology that can detect a signature in the words produced by OpenAI's text-generating AI models. Use cases for this technology include preventing students from using AI to complete their homework, and similar technology is likely to follow in the AI art space with the introduction of cryptographic watermarks inserted into AI-generated images.

While some critics argue that mimicking is part of the natural artistic process and is not necessarily unethical, it's still important to consider the implications of generating art with the precision and scalability that AI permits. For the most part, AI software companies understand and respect this trade-off. They know it is vital to protect the creative rights of existing artists, while also realizing that AI models can produce unique works of art by borrowing from previous styles in a new and exciting way. This represents a fine line and a tightrope that companies active in this space must walk carefully. They must weigh the benefits of technological advancement with the potential consequences of its application. Rather than equip users with the technology to reverse engineer existing works, some degree of randomness will need to be fed into the results—similar to human imperfection. Additionally, software companies need to be able to defend their products against public opinion and navigate complex regulatory environments in order to grow their business.

Perhaps the biggest problem, though, is the lack of clarity and specific oversight designed for this new and emerging field of content creation. As with recent data laws before it, including the General Data Protection Regulation (GDPR) in Europe that requires organizations to obtain consent from individuals before collecting and processing their data, there will be a grey zone for many years as lawyers, ethical bodies, and regulations scramble to catch up with the rapid pace of innovation. In the meantime, the AI creative industry will need to balance policies that respect the intellectual property of individuals while still allowing it to collect data necessary for its growth and development.

16

CONCLUSION

As AI technology develops and adoption expands, it will continue to challenge traditional concepts of artistic expression and redefine what it means to be an artist and content creator.

Using software such as DALL-E or Midjourney, anyone can multiply their design output with little to no budget required and without involving professional human talent. Also, with AI-based tools designed to automate the tedious parts of production, they free up more time for creative steps such as brainstorming, iterating, and experimentation. This offers a new form of leverage that is permissionless; you don't need anyone's permission, cooperation, or investment to start your own creative production line.

Career artists and creative professionals, meanwhile, may find themselves needing to upgrade their skills or move into different roles as AI shoulders more of the creative process—especially on the production side. While AI might be threatening or intimidating, the speed at which this technology is seeping into all aspects of modern content—from voiceovers to book covers—underscores AI content production as a necessary skill for all creators.

I am confident that in the coming years, there will be many opportunities in what the authors of *Human + Machine: Reimagining Work in the Age of AI* term the "missing middle," which is the fertile space where humans and machines collaborate to exploit what each side does best. Machines, for instance, excel at managing large-scale repeatable tasks, while human expertise can help to maintain quality and provide feedback.

In the case of AI art generation, an AI model can be used for spinning up a specific image and the human content creator can use that image as the base for a book cover, YouTube thumbnail, or other content pieces. Using software applications like Canva or Photoshop, the content creator can add the necessary text, edit the dimensions, and make other modifications to produce the final version.

We are already seeing traditional design software including Canva, Notion, and Figma integrate AI text-to-image applications. These features provide users with an all-in-one dashboard for creating visual art, and moving images in the future, starting with three second memes and eventually full-length films.

But for now, have a play around with the AI applications mentioned in this book and keep an eye out for new software solutions and use cases as they emerge. To test out text-to-video AI technology, check out Runway (https://runwayml.com).

Lastly, to keep up with new AI tools, you might like to check out **theresanaiforthat.com** or **futurepedia.io,** which cover a range of categories including art, text, video, and design that you can sort by New, Popular, and Verified.

To access more of my work, please feel free to follow me on Instagram (**machinelearning_beginners**), Skillshare (**www.skillshare.com/user/machinelearning_beginners**), or invest in reading one of the other book titles in this series.

RECOMMENDED RESOURCES

Futurepedia.io

An online resource that covers over 1,000 tools across a range of categories including art, text, video, and design.

The DALL·E Prompt Book

A detailed and free guide to text prompt construction specific to DALL-E.
Link: dallery.gallery/the-dalle-2-prompt-book

Create Stunning AI Art Using Craiyon, DALL-E and Midjourney

Written by Antonis Tsagaris, this was the first book that got me started down the AI art rabbit hole and a resource I recommend to others interested in learning about DALL-E and Midjourney.

Lexica Art

This searchable text prompt library for Stable Diffusion provides a useful reference for inspiration.
Link: lexica.art

Arthub.ai

Another prompt library where you can explore images and prompts from top community artists and designers, including an upvote section.
Link: arthub.art

Theresanaiforthat.com
Lists newly released AI-powered software offerings, mostly in the creative space.

Originality.ai
A plagiarism checker and AI detector built for serious content publishers.

Wire Stock
Upload your AI-generated images to this stock photography platform and earn royalties on sales of your art. You can also explore high-selling images on the platform for inspiration.

OTHER BOOKS BY THE AUTHOR

ChatGPT Prompts Book
Maximize your results with ChatGPT using a series of proven text prompt strategies.

AI for Absolute Beginners
Published in 2023, this book is the complete guide for beginners to AI, including easy-to-follow breakdowns of natural language processing, generative AI, deep learning, recommender systems, and computer vision.

Machine Learning for Absolute Beginners
Learn the fundamentals of machine learning, as explained in plain English.

Machine Learning with Python for Beginners
Progress in ML by learning how to code in Python, build your own prediction models, and solve real-life problems.

Machine Learning: Make Your Own Recommender System
Learn how to make your own ML recommender system in an afternoon using Python.

Data Analytics for Absolute Beginners
Make better decisions using every variable with this deconstructed introduction to data analytics.

Statistics for Absolute Beginners
Master the fundamentals of inferential and descriptive statistics with a mix of practical demonstrations, visual examples, historical origins, and plain English explanations.

SKILLSHARE COURSE

Generative AI Art For Beginners: Midjourney & the Tactics of Killer Text Prompts

Jump into the exciting new field of generative AI art, including all the information and tips you need to start producing your own stunning AI art in minutes.

Made in the USA
Las Vegas, NV
10 April 2025